MARUCA LA CHAPINA

American Girl too

JULIE BAKKER

ISBN 979-8-88832-395-3 (paperback)
ISBN 979-8-88832-396-0 (digital)

Christian Faith Publishing
832 Park Avenue
Meadville, PA 16335
www.christianfaithpublishing.com

Printed in the United States of America

CONTENTS

Preface...v

Introduction..vii

Heroes of the American Continent Conquest...........................ix

    Colonization of the "New Spain"—"New World" xii

    ¡Viva la Independencia! 15 de Septiembre de 1821 xiv

    America—the entire continent's name..............................xiv

    My maternal grandfather: Eugenio Vasquez.......................xv

    My grandmother: Maria Mercedes Zelada de Vasquez xvi

    My mother: Maria Susana Vasques Zelada.......................xvii

Chapter 1: Picking Coffee..1

Chapter 2: Masterpiece..5

Chapter 3: The Scorpion..8

Chapter 4: Planting Corn 10

Chapter 5: The Good News..15

Chapter 6: The Garden of Eden's Procession......................19

Chapter 7: Choosing a Mango from a Tree 23

Chapter 8: Following a Trail..29

Chapter 9: The Beach...33

Chapter 10: Jesus, the Spiritual Light of the Universe 35

Chapter 11: Day of Rest 39

Chapter 12: Patience 44

Chapter 13: National Treasures 48

Bibliography...53

Glosario Guatemalteco...55

Acknowledgments 59

Three hundred eighty-four years from the discovery of the continent, around the year 1876 in Guatemala.

Maruca La Chapina's family history started with her father, Eugenio Vasquez, for this book's purposes. Grandpa Eugenio's last name was derived from a province in Spain called Vasco. No rumor was raised that Grandpa Eugenio was involved in any war in the "New World." By carrying a weapon always, Eugenio protected himself and his family from wild animals, thieves, and murderers on the roads. Maruca also talked about her maternal grandparents who were born in Guatemala; however, no information was necessary to gather for the purposes of this book.

Before Becoming "una República"

History's proof said that the discovery and conquest of the American continent were owed to the adventurous "Spanish Europeans" around the year *1492*. It was as if the sails of Christopher Columbus's ships, without a global positional system (GPS), were being guided with *special winds*, the Holy Spirit winds. After all, it was the planet Earth, where God had its special interest. Spanish sailors could have anchored at the continent of Africa or stopped at the country of India in Asia or stopped in Brazil in South America, Massachusetts in North America, or Japan in Asia; or maybe they could have gone "down and under" to Australia, but *no. That was not in God's plan.*

The winds push them to the *isthmus*, at the center of the *American* continent. The anchorage point of the New World was at the Caribbean Sea (that included all islands). The first island spotted and named by the Spaniards (by C. Columbus) was La Española, which today is known as the Dominican Republic and Haiti, and later the large island of Guantanamo Bay in Cuba became Spain's sea's *base camp*, where all shipments and cargos were brought to the New World, domestic animals such as cows, sheep, horses, pigs, etc. The point of entry to the mainland (continent) was to the territory of "Yucatán," "Campeche," and "Quintana Roo." The New World conquest was at a high price of materials, goods, and human life for both sides. However, through the years, the benefits outweighed the New and Old Worlds.

HEROES OF THE AMERICAN CONTINENT CONQUEST

Guatemala's Indigenous Mayan King and Chief Tecun Uman
Guatemala's Conquistador was the Spanish
Captain Pedro de Alvarado

The conquistador, Captain Hernan Cortez, and his men, after sustaining many battles and confrontations with the inhabitants of the land, had finally entered the land of Chief, Montezuma and camped at the territory. Then, sometime later, Hernan Cortez sent the best captains to gain the territories of Central America. Captain Pedro de Alvarado was sent to the region of what is today Guatemala. However, the news of foreigners coming from another world to invade their land was already in place. In addition, they knew that the foreigners did not want to leave the *newfound paradise*. Native groups in Guatemala were thinking that these foreigners were from another *world*. But many of them knew from the words of the "Mayan" wizards or priests of the coming of these foreigners.

Years before, they had prophesied their coming to the New World. They talked about men with yellow hair in color. The color of the hair was that of the plant called maíz, growing in their land. Their skin color was "pale" and without color, and their eyes were in the color blue, as their blue sky. By then the native groups in Guatemala were not preparing to *welcome* the foreigners. In fact, the Mayan groups were preparing for the worst—they were preparing for war.

Human sacrifices were already conducted for days to pledge their victory over the foreigners. In addition, the great chief, Tecum

Uman, was not going along to war; he was taking his great guerre-ros to defend their land. The nomad native groups on the continent were all different according to the weather conditions and what the land (food) provided to them. The Mayans were polytheists, meaning they had many gods. And their gods required sacrifices of them, animal and human life, depending on the severity and gravity of the request. For example, if the request was for rain on their corn, maybe sacrificing a *jaguar* would do. But if the request, for example, was for the conception of a male—an heir to a cacique, or the assurance of victory in a war—the request required something bigger for the *war god* called Tohil, a human sacrifice (one or many human lives).

The various native indigenous groups were different in their clothing attire, food dishes, tribe wars, annual parties, and hobbies, and they relied on their own administrative laws and for education and religious observations. Tribal wars among the Native Americans were all conducted on foot crossing mountains, ravines, and rivers, carrying their weapons in their hands and backs.

When the great cacique Tecun Uman confronted Captain Pedro de Alvarado, near the river called Usumacinta, he could have observed half of a man on a tall animal with four legs. The horse was a complete *foreigner* to him too. The horse was an animal brought to a New World by the Spaniards. Even though Tecun Uman knew about the *foreigners* in the land and had prepared himself for war by wearing his tribe's war *gala*; dressing with bird's feathers such as long feathers from "quetzals" and "turkeys," jewels of green and black "jade," jaguars' teeth (fangs), and serpent's skins; having markings on his body as skin tattoos; and wearing necklaces of seashells, displaying the riches that the word had given to him.

Tecum Human was armed with [1]a sharp poison spear in one hand, and on the other, he had a large sea-turtle shell used as a shield. On his hand he held a *garrote/club* with sharp stones embedded on both sides of the garrote. On his waist, Tecun had a belt of snakeskins

---

[1]   In a famous Guatemalan painting of the *conquest*, the artist depicted the quetzal bird flying over Uman and Alvarado and his horse at the time of the battle, as if trying to distract Alvarado in order to save the Guatemalan hero's life.

and jaguar's pelt, where knives were hidden and perhaps poisoned darts ready for use. Cap. Pedro de Alvarado was also prepared for war, as ordered by Cortez. He was carrying a shield with the León y Castilla-Carlos V de España's emblem and had a drawn sword. He also carried a black powder rifle; he was wearing a shiny armor suit like an armadillo's cover, and he was also wearing a head shield. Furthermore, Alvarado was mounted on a *war horse*, a horse trained to attack with his front legs and mouth to an opponent warrior. It was mesmerizing for the Indigenous populations of the country to see men riding on horses. But there was no time to think about it; the wizards didn't foretell about these four-legged *creatures*. The war was still going on. Perhaps they thought that it was one single *being*; perhaps Cacique Tecun thought that, if the horse was mortally wounded, the rider was mortally wounded as well. However, at the end of this confrontation, the two powerful men had lost their lives, Cacique Mayan Uman and the Spanish conquistador, Alvarado, along with many more on both sides. Guatemala's history talks about how it was such a bloody massacre that the clear waters of one of Guatemala's rivers, precisely the one named *Usumacinta*, turned red for several days, due to the shedding of blood that occurred at that location.

Then Indigenous fatherless children and weeping women ran away from their towns to the hills and mountains to hide and wait for their future fate, since most of the adventurous people, boarding and working the Spanish ships at that time, were men. Thanks to God and his ultimate control, clergy of the Christian faith (Catholic church) started to defend the Indigenous population (mostly women and children) of their rights as children of God. Indigenous married [2]women were given the last name beside a Christian name: the last name of her husband to be passed on to her children. The last names were precise *names* which originated from the country of Spain, influenced by the location, vocation, or rank of the individual.

Last names were important in Europe, but now, last names were also important in the New World. Last names meant notability and gave a sense of identity, and legitimacy. Children born in the New

____

2

World had a name and two last names; the last name of their father, and the last name of their mother. They were the children born within a married couple in the New World.

The Catholic king and queen, Phillip and Isabella, of Spain decided to economically finance the sea voyages of Christopher Columbus to the New World. However, there was an additional important request made by Queen Isabella to Columbus. Her request was to take the gospel of "Jesus Christ" to the New World as per the Holy Scriptures.

Churches were built in Guatemala as a priority for the first time. A church was like a "fountain of water (eternal water)" of information of the Christian faith for the people. The layout of the church's buildings was to be in the shape of a cross (from the above view). For better understanding to the people, the Bible stories, Jesus's gospel, his life, and passion from his nativity all the way to the cross and resurrection were displayed on wall and ceiling paintings, wall pictures, wood carvings, sculptures, stained glass, and banners. Small bowls containing *holy water* (blessed by clergy) were built at entrances and on each side of the buildings to remind the people of the cleansing power of Jesus's blood and to remind the people of the importance of the blessings through the Trinity (three personas in one God) and baptism (Matthew 28:18–20).

People and especially men were called to behave as responsible gentlemen and obey God's commandments; men were called to love the women (and their children) they had chosen as their wives in holy matrimony and pass on their *last* name to her and their children, just as it was done at their old country of Spain. This is how the making of the new families on the continent started, with the intention of protecting women and their children.

Colonization of the "New Spain"—"New World"

The Catholic Church took an immense role in these social affairs, such as affairs of Judean order and legal law and God's law, urbanization, education, history, agriculture, commerce, and a big important part given to the evangelization of the *people*, per the Catholic Church's rules at the time. All people in Guatemala's land were considered and included "First Americans" known as "Indigenous," "criollos" or people who were born on the continent, "mestizos" or people from parents of Guatemalan (American) and Spanish (European) descent, and lastly other people mainly those who were brought to the continent from Spain.

God's intervention—divine providence. (Luke 24: 46–47)

God used the Spaniard's curiosity and boldness but mainly the political and economic influence that the Catholic king and queen of Spain had on the world during that era to serve his plan. But mainly from the mandates of the "gospel of Jesus Christ," which says that *love* had to superb any other benevolence. The Spaniards had brought to the "New World" gifts and tokens of appreciation with them every time they would return from Europe. People were taught a new language, the Spanish language, but also were taught the Latin language by going to church to worship God and listen to the clergy during mass. People were called Latinos for that reason, and they could use the language used by the clergy. Also, domestic animals such as horses, cows, sheep, and chickens were brought to the New World and those which were considered to be domestic, such as pigs, oxen, and bulls. Among plants, the Spaniards also brought wheat, oats, almonds, and others. Once the news of the existence of a "New World" was made known to the rest of Europe and the world, more people started to come to the New World, and this raised uneasiness for the people of the "New World," especially Native Americans, and for many of them, peace had not arrived to the New World from Europe. On the contrary, people from other countries traveled to the "New World" to seek fortunes and other riches found in the New World's natural resources.

English Europeans had anchored at the New World at the area we now know as Massachusetts in the United States around the year *1620*. One hundred fifty-six (156) years later, the people of the United States obtained and signed its independence from England on *July 4, 1776*.

¡Viva la Independencia! 15 de Septiembre de 1821

Guatemala's founding fathers, José Cecilio del Valle (attorney-at-law), Juan Beltran, and others, had obtained and signed their independence from Spain three hundred twenty-nine (329) years later, on *September 15, 1821*. It became a sovereign republic. Guatemala's people have always been known for being *hospitable* for obvious reasons (temperature, great natural resources, variety of food, the meekness of its people, etc.). Then, secondly, allegedly, the country of England under pretense, lies, and deceitfulness overpowered Guatemala and misappropriated the land of Belize. Ironically, later on, the territory of Belize obtained its independence from England as well.

Well, despite all these past events—Guatemala's history from back then until today—Guatemala continues to be a republic with its neighbors of Mexico, Belize, El Salvador, and Honduras.

America—the entire continent's name

The name of the continent was owed to Americo Vespucio who was able to follow the route of Christopher Columbus and go beyond to explore more of the entire continent. He followed the seashore, the south part of the continent—rich and fertile lands, comfortable weather and climate, the certainty of finding food, fewer risks of tropical storms, and more.

Maruca La Chapina's family history started with her father, Eugenio Vasquez, for this book's purposes. Grandpa Eugenio's last name referred to a province in Spain called Vasco. No rumor was raised that Grandpa Eugenio was involved in any war in the "New World." By carrying a weapon always, Eugenio protected himself and his family from wild animals, thieves, and murderers on the roads. Maruca also talked about her maternal grandparents who were born in Guatemala; however, no information was necessary to gather for the purposes of this book.

My maternal grandfather: Eugenio Vasquez

Fifty-five (55) years, after Guatemala's independence from Spain, Eugenio Vasquez, Maruca La Chapina's father, was born in Guatemala around the year *1876*. Eugenio was living in one of the "best agricultural regions" in the country—fertile soil and adequate rainfall. In addition, with its tropical climate, it is one of the best-growing areas in the world. Young Eugenio had already his dream alive in him. He was born in the New World ("el nuevo mundo"). Some said the name of the New World for the new continent was "Colombia"; others gave the credit to the word *America*. However, Eugenio was a peaceful man, not a politician nor a revolutionary man. He wanted to be a landowner ("terrateniente"). He was just a hardworking man who loved a woman, Mercedes; a man who wanted a family with children and who wanted a piece of "terruno de tierra" (land).

Eugenio used his God-given strength and dedication to work during the harvest seasons only; after all, he took great care of his hands, for his artistic and carpentry works. Eugenio had the opportunity to work for large growers during the harvest seasons chopping sugarcane and picking coffee and corn, chocolate, and other fruits. Many of these crops were for exportation and supported Guatemala's economy. Eugenio learned to enjoy and appreciate the fruits of the harvest and to thank God for his great fortune. Because of his good reputation as a reliable and conscientious worker, Eugenio had no problems finding work during the harvest season. He was a man that enjoyed riding horses to get to one location from another one in a relatively fast way.

He owned a "muzzleloader" (gun) that he loaded with gunpowder and "lead" bullets with the help of a "ramrod." Eugenio used his gun for personal defense and to hunt animals for food. Also, he ensured that his working tools were kept clean, sharp, and ready to use when needed as his several "machetes," especially, when he worked at the sugarcane farms—working at sugarcane farms with a "dull machete" was a big mistake. In addition, many times, Eugenio had used his machete to defend himself from snakes that frequented nesting among the immature stalks of sugarcane, while cutting tallos (sugarcane stalks).

However, Eugenio's skillful abilities were in "artistic carpentry." He designed and shaped wood to create beautiful and decorative pieces to adorn the outside of "corner windows" and doors mainly at churches, cathedrals, and other important houses in the "old" Guatemala's capital city—Antigua, Guatemala.

My grandmother: Maria Mercedes Zelada de Vasquez

Maruca's mother was born around the year 1890. Maruca's maternal grandparents were owners of a store (tienda de campo) in Escuintla, Guatemala. The items that were available to buy perhaps were ropes, baskets, needles and threads, cotton products, hats, some fruits such as coconuts and bananas, sugarcane stalks for chewing, pork's lard, soap balls (made out of ashes and lard), rice, beans and don't forget alcoholic drinks including "cusha," a Mayan alcoholic drink, and beer (cerveza "gallo").

Mercedes Zelada was harvesting the benefits of the *integration* of the West and East worlds. As a complete, *fresh* musical composition or as a balanced chemical equation of two kingdoms, American Indigenous and Spanish Europeans (from the America and Europe continents), Mercedes was a lucky girl! She was very fortunate of having a Christian Catholic father and family who loved her. She was happy to be "criolla." She was a Mestiza-Latina. But furthermore, she knew that she had a "heavenly Father," who loved her very much.

Mercedes was born in the small country of Guatemala. The country of Guatemala was full of natural resources such as mountains, rivers, lakes, volcanos, and valleys; the several mountain ranges such as the Sierra Madre. The mountain range started in Alaska and went all the way through the American continent until the southern part of the continent, between the countries of Argentina and Chile ("tierra del fuego"). The Spaniards wanted to ensure their presence on the new continent by leaving a mark—the land was beautiful and immense and they were few. Precisely, by naming their new discoveries with a Spanish name/word, they would ensure at least some kind of ownership or belonging. Rumors said that the first of the series of mountain peaks were "Sierra Madrid" as the name of the capital of the country of Spain. Then, after time and mispronunciation of the name, it was just left with the name "Sierra Madre."

My mother: Maria Susana Vasques Zelada

Maruca La Chapina was born in May of the year *1924*, and Maruca belonged to one of the generations that enjoyed the benefits of the blend of God's laws and men's laws. But above all, Maruca La Chapina was now a member of a new kingdom now baptized belonging to God's kingdom. Also, Maruca was fortunate to have a Christian Catholic and apostolic man as a father. Maruca was happy to be a "ladina" or "mestiza; to be "ladina" in Guatemala meant to be part "Indigenous Native American" and part "Spanish." The name Maruca was derived from the name "Maria." However, Maruca didn't appreciate being called by the name Maria; she knew that Jesus's mother's name was "Santa Maria." The name Maria was recognized in the "New World" as an appropriate name for a girl born in the "New World" too.

Maruca La Chapina was a rich girl in "culture and history," a brand-new type of "genetic material." In addition, she was born into a family of an "artistic" father, a field harvest worker, but the family also worked the land they owned. A family who attended the Christian Roman Catholic church in their town. Her father worked for the church creating specialized wooden pieces on windows and doors.

Maruca liked to wear cotton, plain-colored, long, and puffy dresses. She enjoyed occasionally running barefoot, burying and cooling her toes in the dirt during hot days. She liked to scratch with her hands the edges of the river banks for mollusks and other crustaceans to add to the "mariscos soup" made at home by her mom.

She liked to gather trees and vegetation, sticks, branches, and debris to help with the cooking fire. She also liked to gather herbs, spices, roots, and other digestible vegetables to take to mom.

Corn products continued to be important in Maruca's family food diet, products such as tortillas (corn), tamales and atol de elote.

Maruca La Chapina liked to speak the Spanish language, but she also liked to speak words in the Mayan Quiché language and could communicate with merchants and other people at the market, church, plaza, and other places.

Maruca would refer to her "heavenly Father" when she was a child as her *tata*, a Native American word for God creator.

Maruca La Chapina was a very educated girl of the world surrounding her, unschooled beyond second grade for reasons beyond her control, but she was coached and instructed by her parents, her older brother, and clergy of the church. The standard level of education in her day and place was elementary school. Also, being the only daughter in the family, she had to help mama at home. Maruca La Chapina started going to school in her town around the year 1930.

The school system in Guatemala in those days, like many school classrooms in North and South America, were set up to have all school children in town, regardless of their age and gender, in one classroom. Maximiliano, Maruca's brother, was in the same classroom too. Two years later, one day in the classroom, Maruca being a good, observant child, when the students were writing and making loud noises on their small chalkboards with their "chalks"/lead sticks, Maruca lifted her head up and saw her male teacher behaving in a way that was questionable of his authority over school-age children. An insult to the profession of "pedagogy."

The teacher had his hand under a young girl's blouse and was caressing the student's chest. The student was one of Maruca's classmates—an older girl. However, the intriguing part of this event was that the school teacher had noticed Maruca observing his behavior. Then, somehow, the teacher felt embarrassed and stopped misbehaving, according to Maruca. But by then it was too late for her, as first, she had become a *witness* to a school employee's potential *felony* that could ruin his reputation as a school teacher. Of course, Maruca did not want to take part in any such *disgrace* so early in life, while going to school to learn the *a, b, c*'s of the Spanish language. Second, this embarrassing experience made an impression on Maruca's mind that she never forgot.

After school, Maruca La Chapina told her parents at home what she had observed at school. Eugenio, being the head of the household, discussed the matter with Mercedes and brought it to God with prayer. After that, they had decided to take it to school and inform them of it. On their return home, Eugenio and Mercedes called up Maruca and told her that they needed to discuss if Maruca should continue going to the town's school that year. Eugenio and Mercedes had decided that Maruca would stop going to school that year. Max continued going to school. He was seated at the back of the classroom and had not paid attention to the teacher's conduct.

Soon after, rumors spread that the school teacher had left the school and town. Maruca La Chapina, being young and knowing that her parents loved her and wanted the best for her, stayed close to her parents and obeyed them.

However, this situation did not stop Maruca La Chapina from developing her curiosity and learning capabilities (knowledge) to know about the universe created by her Tata, surrounding her with people who loved and appreciated her.

Maruca's parents would take her to church on Sundays to know God better. The good news was that Jesus Christ was enough for "salvation" and the door to "Heaven," the real paradise. A love's mystery. Maruca's mother had planted the seed of "faith in God" in her children since they were very young. Fortunately, Maruca La Chapina was married in God's will to a man who was going to love her and wanted the best for her. She became his lawfully wedded wife, and with love and trust, Maruca was able to learn reading and writing in the Spanish language. However, there were some steps he was able to take to guide her together.

- *First,* he taught her the "Roman alphabet" in the Spanish language. The Roman alphabet in the Spanish language has a total of twenty-nine (29) letters, five (5) of them are vowels, and twenty-four (24) are consonants; the additional letters in the alphabet are: double *r* ("RR"), double *l* ("LL"), and the letter *ñ*.

Other letters in the Roman alphabet in the Spanish language include the letter *y*, borrowed from the Greek alphabet, and it is known as *y* (Greek). The letter *i* is known in the Spanish language as *i* (latina que anteriormente reemplaza la letra *j* también, especialmente en pronunciación). A good classical example of this letter is the sign, posted on the cross of Jesus Christ when he was crucified. The governor, Pontius Pilate, mandated the posting of the abbreviation "INRI" which meant, "Jesus of Nazareth, King of the Jews" (Mark 15:26, Luke 23:38, John 19:19, plus Matthew 27:37).

- *Second*, he taught her about the correct "pronunciation" (phonics) of all letters of the Spanish language alphabet and how to connect letters, syllables, and words with the correct sound and pronunciation. He told her that all letters in the alphabet were important, all of them counted, and none of them were ignored. The letters had a unique "sound," just like the "keys" on a "marimba" the musical instrument, or the "cords" on a wooden Spanish guitar, that when combined together, would create "sweet melodies" but with one (1) letter. This letter was silent. This letter had to be present in the word. This one letter was the letter *H*. For example, as in the word *honor*. *Honor* God, *honor* your parents, and *honor* your country. Perhaps, this notion helped Maruca La Chapina, to decide later on, when her employer proposed her to move (live) with them to San Francisco, California, USA. Her employer valued Maruca's work ethics and considered her a member of the family. However, she declined the invitation and decided to remain in her beautiful country of Guatemala with her fiancé, Francisco (1949), with the idea of establishing a home together. Later on, the family "Calderon Zelada" was legally formalized and decided to build their first house in Guatemala City, Guatemala.

- *Third,* he taught her the study of "calligraphy" (penmanship), the art of producing fancy writing. This item was very important to know and execute for both (Francisco and Maruca) because Maruca was going to learn to sign important legal documents of their life together as husband and wife. Legal documents such as their civil wedding certificate, land and property deeds, children's birth certificates (child's name with father's last name first and mother's last name second), vehicle's titles, cemetery plot title rights, and other legal documents that require a legal and valid signature.

Consequently, Maruca's education in the Spanish language was enriched, and she learned how to write, sign her name, and ultimately how to read. However, Maruca La Chapina never changed her mind when it came to her professional vocation in the "culinary arts." She would always impress her family and friends with her cooking creations, without following long-written recipes.

At the town plaza was also the place where Maruca talked to other people, who knew Maruca's family, to learn Spanish. She would hear about other issues and news about what was happening in town. The plaza's church was the place where one could hear words in Spanish and other languages used in the Bible. Maruca would confirm the teachings from Mama and Papa—teachings on fearing, obeying, and loving God unconditionally. Also, at the plaza's market, Maruca would hear new words in the Mayan Quiché language.

At the plaza was where people would plan the church's annual parties/festivities. Also, people could listen to marimba music melodies accompanied by drums, recorders, flutes, cymbals, and rattles, which was an excellent distraction for the entire family. On occasions, people would *dance* (bailar) on the streets to show their happiness and content. "Vamos al baile."

CHAPTER 1

Picking Coffee

Maruca La Chapina liked to help her father at work when her father would allow her. Maruca's father was as a "carpenter," an artistic carpenter. His main creations and designs were the wooden pieces to be placed on "corner windows" on buildings of the "old" Guatemala's capital city—Antigua, Guatemala. When his "artistic wooden projects" were completed, he would supplement his income by harvesting at fields of coffee, sugar, and corn farms by the Pacific Ocean.

When Eugenio would work at the coffee farms sometimes, Maruca La Chapina would accompany him to work at the coffeebush; she would help him to remove the coffee grains on the lower branches of the coffee plant. Maruca knew a lot about harvesting coffee grains; she knew how to recognize the "ripe" grains; she knew how to carefully remove grains without bursting the other grains on the branch or damaging the not-yet-ripe and the green grains on the branch and fill her basket full.

One day, Eugenio decided to take Maruca to work with him. Happily, Maruca got up early that day; she filled her "water container" with fresh water. In a bag for their lunch, she took some "corn product" prepared at home the night before, along with "cooked yuca with some pork meat and tomato sauce" and wrapped it in "banana leaves" and dos bananas. Eugenio prepared their "wagon" attached to their horse named "Flecha" for their trip to the coffee farm going on the roads that were familiar to Eugenio.

Then, that day at the farm, Maruca wanted to show her dad that she could and was able to work by herself on a "coffeebush" alone; so she convinced Eugenio, and Eugenio looked and chose a "small coffeebush" for Maruca, Eugenio's "little princess." However, the location of this coffeebush was a little far away from where Eugenio was working at the farm. To Maruca's surprise, when she was lowering a branch with her hand to remove the coffee grains, she saw a serpent with brown-grayish color and diamond patterns on her back. It was sitting coiled up around the center of the "coffeebush" and making a sound with her tail—shaking its rattle. Its length was approximately six to seven feet long. The serpent was doing what other serpents know how to do, with its tongue—it was sensing the conditions of the environment, such as the temperature of the radiant energy from a "live human body," and it was looking at Maruca La Chapina.

Maruca, astonished and frightened, backed away without words to say. Slowly and carefully, she let go of branch without making a commotion to hurt the serpent and ran to look for her father. When she got to the place where her dad was working with a coffeebush, Eugenio did not have an idea of what could have frightened Maruca so badly. Maruca was her only daughter, and he loved her very much; she was the only female who had survived the tragedy of their children.

Maruca and Max were the only survivors of thirteen (13) children; sad to say, eleven (11) children did not live past the age of two (2) years old. Eugenio was happy to know that he had two living children, and he wanted to help them both. Eugenio was thankful to God for granting life to his family—a wife, a son, and a daughter living near the Pacific Ocean in Guatemala, Central America.

Then Maruca, who was standing there without any audible words, started to communicate with her father by making the "hand signs" they both knew. The hand sign of "an animal" and the hand sign of "a plant." Then Eugenio understood from the signs that Maruca made that she had seen an animal in the coffeebush and quickly went to where Maruca was working to confirm her "state of alarm."

Eugenio knew about reptiles and most definitely about the snakes in the area, which was abundant in vegetation and water. On several occasions he had taken snakes to their house, so Mercedes could serve it as a meal for the family. He saw the reptile and said to himself, *Oh, a rattle* (chinchin), so he unsheathed his sharp "machete" and decapitated the snake. The workers at the farm were happy to know that Eugenio had killed the "serpent" in the coffeebush and that he had decided to keep the serpent's body and take it home to Mercedes to be served at mealtime for the family. At that time, snakes were considered a delicacy.

After this incident, Maruca La Chapina was told by Eugenio that she couldn't come back to help Eugenio to gather coffee beans at the farm unless she worked beside Eugenio on the same coffeebush. Maruca was obedient to her parents, and Maruca obeyed and loved her parents. Maruca La Chapina liked to listen when the "padre" would recite the Ten Commandments that were given to "people" from God and were about shaping people's behavior and conduct. The fifth commandment was most special for Maruca because it talks about "giving honor" to our parents. The book of Ephesians talks about "the promise of the right thing to do is obey our parents…because God has placed them in authority over us."

Mercedes told her daughter that she had not been very obedient to her mom and dad in the past. She left the home to go with Eugenio to start a family. Mercedes, La Chapina's mom, had everything at her reach—having a mom, a dad, and a maternal grandmother, and everything else a "young lady" could ever dream of having during that time. She left it all because she wanted to form her "own" unadulterated home as God mandated between a man and a woman with Eugenio even though she was only fifteen years old.

Counting only on God's blessings, Mercedes decided to take on the great responsibilities that would come with the adventures of following your own heart. Maruca's mom had decided to pay attention to the idea that she could form a "home" with the man whom she had fallen in love with. Eugenio had behaved like a "gentleman" to her, and he had made her feel as "beautiful and interesting" as a "young maiden" could be. Maruca's mom continued telling Maruca that—thanks be to God—the day came when Maruca La Chapina's family, her grandparents and parents, reconciled their differences. They said apologetic words toward each other to express with mutual understanding and peace between them to continue living their lives with God's blessings without regrets. Eugenio had given plenty of evidence to his in-laws that he really loved Maruca's mom and their children, Max and Maruca.

CHAPTER 2

Masterpiece

Maruca's father enjoyed working as an "artistic" carpenter; he knew that he needed his hands to work to create his distinguished creations. His hands and mind were trained to create masterpieces at the house of God—churches at Antigua, Guatemala. Eugenio had the necessary skills to ensure that his "pieces of work" had the exact dimensions to fit precisely. Eugenio had to fabricate intricate wooden moldings to fit into the rough stone/masonry window openings.

Eugenio's land had three main buildings at his "terruno de tierra," The home was to the west-south corner; it had sleeping quarters, a kitchen, and an attached woodshed. The woodshop building was at the southwest corner of the property and had no connections to any corridors or the house. The frontage wall of the property had a portal ("porton"), a large door where the carriage/horse could enter and keep. Behind it was a corridor that went to the left and connected to the home. The barn building was located on the northwest corner of the property. The carpentry building was where he kept all his completed work and "tools" such as nails, saws, hammers, drills, chisels, sharp stones, a carpenter's square, a working table with a flat surface, and spare lumber.

On several occasions, Maruca and her brother liked to visit the carpentry shop. To the children, it was like entering a new world, because it was kept close to them most of the time. They would go to play and see what their father had in the building. They liked to play with the sawdust and small pieces of wood or just observe their father work on a piece of wood and observe the making of curves and turns on "raw wood," seeing that Eugenio's clean hands would quickly turn powdery and sandy. However, work and visits to the carpentry shop had to be during the daylight. Eugenio kept candles in the room, but they were hardly used. He preferred to work in the brightness of the day. There was no electricity on those days, and people worked during the day time, even before the first beam of light had entered the eastern sky until sundown. People rested at night. Therefore, Eugenio liked to keep his shop locked and secured.

One stormy and rainy afternoon, Maruca and her brother accompanied their father to the carpentry shop. Then, when the three of them were occupied with details of piles of sawdust on the dirt floors, while Eugenio was sweeping and picking up dust from the ground, gray clouds were crowding the sky and moving rapidly, along with flashing lights and loud sounds. Then, in an instant, the carpentry shop was illuminated with a tremendous flash of light—all was as bright and clear like having a room with no roof on a sunny day, all exposed to the heavens. There were no secrets in the carpentry room, not even under the pile of sawdust on the floor, and it was only approximately mid-afternoon.

The shock of the "brilliant light" knocked them off their feet, blind and deaf, and made them close their eyes. Because at the same time, in a fraction of a second, the bright light was followed by a deafening noise of "thunder." Luckily, probably because the ground being a dirt floor, it absorbed the shock of the force, preventing Max, Maruca, and Eugenio from sustaining serious injuries. Then, trembling, they opened their eyes and thanked God for their fate. They stood up from the floor; Eugenio picked Maruca up and held her in his arms closer than he ever. Eugenio grabbed Max's hand and walked out of the carpentry room. They were just surprised and amazed by God's power and his creation's wonders. Eugenio expressed out loud his thanks to God, and at the same time, he took time to look at his children and enjoy the feeling of seeing them well and alive.

Perhaps, the carpentry shop had to be rebuilt, the roof and walls had to be reconstructed, and the finished wood pieces had to be redone because although they were not burned by the force of the lightning, they were soaked in rainwater. But most importantly Eugenio and his children were not hurt or harmed. Maruca already knew that there would be lightning; before the rain, she have seen the strikes of lightning in the sky, and later she heard the loud thunders. That was what the rainy season like when living near the Pacific Ocean in Guatemala, Central America. But maybe, she did not understand the specific scientific details of what had happened at her father's "carpentry shop"; the speed of light is greater than the speed of sound (C speed of light in a vacuum = 3.00×10^8 m/s); the different electric charges between the planet and its atmosphere; the type of clouds visible before the rain, such as nimbus; and the temperatures of the air currents. However, Maruca La Chapina knew that rainwater was essential for plants to grow to be converted into food for consumption, and rainwater was fundamental for supporting the life of animals and people on the planet.

Most importantly, Maruca La Chapina was glad and thankful to go back to the artistic carpentry shop once again to play sawdust and wood with her brother. Perhaps, she pretended the pieces of wood were members of a family similar to hers. Maruca and her brother were young, but they were learning life lessons. God's love for them, having a father near them to hug during scary and rainy afternoons, powerful natural forces, and rebuilding the carpentry shed after the lightning strike—surely, all these experiences helped Maximiliano to decide to follow in his father's footsteps in becoming a carpenter later on in life.

CHAPTER 3

The Scorpion

Maruca La Chapina liked to play the children's game called hide-and-seek with her brother, Max. She loudly counted the numbers one through ten, and her brother would go to hide some place at their property. When she was done counting, Maruca would go and find her brother. Once Maruca would find her brother, in game hide-and-seek, they would switch roles, and she would be the one who'd have to hide from her brother.

One day while they were playing this game, Maruca went to hide in the woodshed behind the house, where the family kept firewood for cooking the meals. The firewood room was exactly behind their kitchen, a rectangular-shaped room with three walls and a roof. The cut wood was kept dry, warm, and ready to use.

At this time, Maruca could have hidden in the barn, even though it was farther from where Maximiliano was counting out loud. The barn had more places to hide, and besides, there was hay and other grains (dry corn, beans, and rice). Some animals in the barn could have been quiet like the oxen or the horses. But between the chickens and Nero, the guardian dog, they would surely give her hiding place away.

So Maruca decided to hide in the woodshed. The woodshed did not have any windows, just one side open with no door. So she quickly went in and tried to stand on top of a freshly cut pile of wood. While Maruca was trying to balance her sandaled feet on logs of wood, catching her regular breathing, and calming herself down from the excitement, she felt something sharp on her right ankle that made her scream. Maruca's eyes went down to her right foot and saw an enormous menacing black scorpion (aracnidos) with its stinger still up in the air scurrying over the logs of wood and going out of the room.

Maruca screamed again and took a couple of steps down to the dirt floor. Mercedes was in the kitchen preparing food when she heard Maruca's screams. Then Maruca's family heard her loud cries and ran to aid her. Maruca's mother and father went to make "health" remedies based from what they learned from their parents and grandparents, such as salt ($NaCl$/sodium chloride) from the Pacific Ocean, lemon juice or sour orange juice, rubbing alcohol (ethyl alcohol/CH_2H_5OH) to disinfect the wound, and chlorophyll liquid from aloe vera plant to repair the skin tissues.

Maruca, who received loving care from her family, stayed in bed for approximately a week. She had symptoms such as high fever, skin inflammation on her ankle, redness of the skin, and depleted energy. Thank God, relatively a few days after that, Maruca started to feel better, and very soon the inflammation and the redness of the skin disappeared. Then Maruca La Chapina went back to get firewood from the woodshed again to help her mother to cook the family's meals. She knew that the woodshed was a "refuge" from the rain and cold for small animals such as rabbits and chickens. But now Maruca understood that "arachnids" like the scorpion, who stung her a couple of times at the woodshed, also enjoyed the security of the woodshed.

CHAPTER 4

Planting Corn

Everyone in the Vasquez-Zelada family had duties and obligations to do at home, regardless of their age and gender, and even more so when Maruca's mom didn't have a "helper" on the household chores. Maruca La Chapina had to help her mother when preparing the family's meals. She had to help clean and prepare a pot of "black beans," clean and cook corn, prepare "chicken meal," gather the dirty laundry, and wash laundry at the town's basin of *pila* (Mayan word, *guacal*) with a bowl.

The word *pila* is an example of the Roman Empire's influence on the Spanish language vocabulary in the country of Guatemala and that still prevails to this day. The concept of such a word was introduced by the Spaniards to the New World. Pontius Pilate washed his hands publicly to demonstrate his verdict on the innocence of Jesus, who was falsely accused" (Luke 23: 13–14). The word *pila(s)* in Guatemala means a place where water can be found with a volume of approximately twenty to thirty gallons of water (H_2O). Pilas are found in private households or in public places (free of charge). They are cast concrete pieces with a large tank to hold and keep water for use. In addition, the pila has places to place objects to be washed or cleaned. Water from a well can be extracted and used to drink, wash laundry, wash food, and wash dishes.

When there was no one at home to grind the corn manually, the cooked corn had to be taken to the town's mill, so Maruca's mom could make tortillas. Maruca also helped to gather the harvest in their family's garden (onions, tomatoes, guisquiles, ayotes, and other vegetables). Maruca La Chapina had to feed the chickens when no one else could do it, but what she enjoyed doing very much was gathering the eggs from the chicken coop at their stable where large animals (four-footed mammals) were kept along with their "guardian" dog, Nero. Maruca's mom would be there to help her to accomplish the job when she couldn't finish the work required. However, when Maruca's mom had an accident with one of the family's oxen (four-footed bovine mammals) in the field while plowing and sowing the ground to plant corn, it rushed Maruca to take on more responsibilities than ever at home. Maruca La Chapina was the only "female" who worked the household chores along with her mother. The corn had to go in the ground, but before that, the soil had to be tilled and broken and be free from weeds, before the rainy season.

Mercedes, Maruca La Chapina's mother, would guide the team of oxen by a rope tied to the "brass" rings that were placed in the oxen's noses, leading them in the direction she wanted them to go and pulling the plow behind, while the oxen were pulling the plow. Eugenio needed to be behind the oxen guiding the plow as the plow tilled the soil. The oxen were of Brahman breed, and some of their characteristics are the following: they had long horns, they are usually docile, they stand about five feet tall at the shoulder, they weigh between 1,000 and 1,500 pounds, and they easily adapted to the climate of Escuintla, Guatemala, which is hot and humid (H&H).

That day, the oxen were not feeling very docile and cooperative and didn't want to work with Mercedes, or maybe because the flies were irritating them. When the oxen reached the end of their property, Mercedes pulled on the rope to turn the oxen to go in the opposite direction. An ox shook his head and accidentally gashed her side with one of his large horns. Mercedes screamed out in pain; she grabbed her stomach with both hands and fell to her knees on the ground.

Maruca's father was horrified to see his wife kneeling and bleeding from the abdomen. He rushed to be by her to soothe the pain of being harmed by the clumsiness of a beast, leaving all behind carelessly at the planting field, the animals, the planting seeds of corn, and his farming tools. Eugenio hastily removed his dusty apron from his waist, threw it on the ground, saw the wounded area on Mercedes's body, and carried her in his arms to the house to give her first aid.

This was completely unexpected—the ox had been a "great help" to Eugenio in previous years and this was just an unfortunate accident; the ox never intended to hurt Mercedes. Now, Mercedes was wounded, crying, and in a serious condition. Eugenio laid Mercedes on their wedding bed, kneeling by the bed, with his eyes saturated in tears and fixed on the "crucifix" that was hanging just above the bed's headboard, Eugenio started to pray for his wife's life. He mumbled words, words from the "Lord's Prayer" (Luke 11:2–4). He thought, *Thank God, her wound entry was the deepest to one side, and it continued without perforating a vital organ.* Then Eugenio got up and started to get the "home remedies" he knew from before. The natural home remedies were salt (NaCl) from the Pacific Ocean; Eugenio knew that salt was used to preserve meats; lemon juice and alcohol (ethyl alcohol /C_2H_5OH) were helpful for disinfecting too.

Most importantly, Eugenio was brave and able to medically care for his woman, his wife, the mother of his children, when she needed it the most. This was not the very first time, because he had provided her with help during the times she gave birth to their children. When the town's midwife would not make it on time to Vasquez-Zelada's home, Eugenio would the one who would help her to catch/hold the "baby." On very few occasions, Eugenio would cut the "umbilical cord" to free their children from their mother's uterus, wipe clean their babies' noses and mouths after birth, to ensure their own breathing of atmospheric air containing oxygen (O_2), nitrogen (N), carbon monoxide (CO_2), argon (Ar), and more. This fact was very important in the life of these children—"earthling" babies. After agreeing with Mercedes on a specific name to give to their babies, he would wrap his children and hold them for the first time—all this without any medical education but with lots of love and faith in God, the giver of life. Then Eugenio would wait for the midwife to get to his house and take over his baby and wife.

In regards to the accident with the ox, Eugenio knew that this was something unique, once in a lifetime. Mercedes's baby deliveries had been "normal," meaning they were "vaginal deliveries," not cesarean sections (C—named after the Roman emperor Julius Cesar). This accident with the ox had ripped not only Mercedes's epidermis—the outside layer of skin—but also the dermis—the inner layer of the skin—as well as muscle tissue layers and fatty tissue layers. Regardless of the medical diagnosis, the wound had to be dressed and had to be protected from infection.

In addition, Eugenio knew how to wrap rather than to sew or fasten by stitches. He would carefully wrap his finished "wood pieces" and place them on the horse-wagon to be taken to Guatemala's capital city—back then, Antigua—to later install them in their appropriate place. He would tie his animals (four-footed mammals) at his barn when needed; he would tie his dog, Nero, at a permanent place to keep his property's yard free from Nero's smelly droppings.

Eugenio also knew that Mercedes was better at giving stitches; she was very handy with threads and needles. She would make clothing for the family. This time, however, she had been injured, and she was bedridden. Eugenio looked for alcohol around the house; he found a bottle of "guaro" (a drink made out of sugarcane similar to rum), La Quetzalteca, and some clean cotton sheets and started dressing Mercedes's wound. He cleaned the wounded area; first, he simply washed it with soap and water and disinfected it with guaro. He pulled the torn skin, muscles, and fatty layers; bound them together; and tied them firmly with a ribbon to form a knot. Then he wrapped Mercedes's lower abdomen area with clean cotton sheets; he gave Mercedes a drink of alcohol to dull her pain and calm her sensibility. When Eugenio noticed that Mercedes was calming down, he sent Maximiliano, their son, on a horse-wagon to town to find the "wise midwife" for help.

Also, the news of Mercedes's accident was given to the church's priest and soon the church's family started to offer help too; people offered prepared meals, visits to Mercedes, and prayers at the church for healing. Maruca La Chapina's family was known and recognized in their town.

However, even with the great help from their town, Maruca was able to pull her weight at home while still being only ten years old.

The accident gave them opportunities for Maruca to learn how to make a pot of black beans with an herb called apasote for the family—with coaching from her father, Eugenio. In addition, instead of making tortillas, Maruca learned how to make tamalitos de masa with "chipilín" (garden herb)—a corn-dough-based product—to nourish the family. Fresh tortillas required experience from well-trained hands. Maruca had not developed the skill, yet.

Maruca La Chapina was able to demonstrate that with faith in God, all members in a family regardless of their age—as Maruca's family had during an accident with an ox—could help to benefit the entire family.

This experience in Maruca La Chapina's life influenced her to decide to go into the "culinary" arts as her chosen profession for her life. She enjoyed preparing dishes from several recipes and several other countries, but that is another story.

Maruca's mother, Mercedes, day by day regained her stamina more and more until one day, she pulled through completely and was able to do her job as a mother in the Vasquez-Zelada's family. Eugenio and Mercedes gave thanks to God again for Mercedes's recovered health, so both of them could continue caring for their family, with their children, Max and Maruca, living in Escuintla, Guatemala.

CHAPTER 5

The Good News

While Maruca La Chapina was learning and growing in the world around her, she appreciated the difference between people and animals. On Sundays, the church's priest would talk about the word of God: God the father's love for humanity; of the disobedience—original sin—of the first human couple created by God, our ancestors Adam and Eve; and the way that God had planned to reconcile "humanity" to him; his creation.

All humans/earthlings—young, old, men, women, girls, and boys—were marked with the word *sinner*. This made humanity feel isolated and away from God, and while attempting to stay near God, humanity made a lot of sacrifices, great works, and deeds of reconciliation with God. However, compared to God's perfection and holiness, humanity's deeds are just as "dirty rags." They didn't have any value toward the person's salvation—personal salvation. But God's plan was unparalleled; he had decided to reconcile his creation to him. It had to be a "perfect sacrifice" pleasing to him, the Creator. It had to be unique, one of a kind, and one for all who believed in God's "mystery of salvation." It had to be a holy" being," one without the mark of "sin," superior to humans or earthlings.

Like a gardener, God made a "graft" on the planet earth at the molecular/nucleic acids level (DNA). A graft is the joining of one single branch to a branch of an existent bush; for example, the tying of a small-white-petaled rose's branch to a large-pink-petaled rose's bush, resulting in roses with bigger petals, of white and pink colors. The savior of humanity had to be fully God (divine) and fully human—Jesus, the rose of heaven.

However, God's plan had several requirements, starting with the requirement of a conception of this being. The conception had to take place in the "uterus" of a young virgin—a "virgin" in all meanings of the word, without any insertion of x-, y-, and z-planes—mental, physical, and emotional stages. The other requirement in God's plan for being the "savior of humanity" would be that he had to be "male" in his human form because he is the Son of God before Creation. He had to be a "gentleman" and not a "lady" (Luke 1:26–38).

Then God grafted himself into "humanity" in the form of a "baby boy"—an "earthling." How precious, a personal savior! An earthling with a father and mother (Joseph and Mary) who cared for him while young living on "planet earth." God's son would be falsely accused and have a horrible death on a wooden cross. But this was not the ultimate requirement; there was another requirement, a "divine" requirement. The son of God couldn't stay buried forever. The son of God would be resurrected in three (3) days, even though the tomb where he was laid was new, unused.

Later, he would visit hell (a place without God), and then Jesus would appear alive showing his (hands and chest) wounds to his earthling followers. Then, after forty (40) days after his resurrection, Jesus would ascend into heaven (breaking the force of gravity that is 9.8 meters per second squared without the use of rocket fuel) and would present himself to God, his father. The mission would be accomplished. Moreover, God's plan included not leaving us alone, because the Holy Spirit—God's spirit—would stay with us (John 1:49).

However, more information could be found in a book called the Bible. Maruca La Chapina was appreciative of God's love and liked going to church on Sundays to celebrate Jesus Christ's death and resurrection and sing songs proclaiming the hope of his returning to the planet. God the Father had spoken there were no doubts and there was no second-guessing, when introducing Jesus, his son, to people from the planet (Matthew 3:16–17). Surely, the most important "good news" was that the Messiah had come to earth—no more waiting. God made his introduction with no apologies, the most important "good news" in the Bible.

The priest explained that God had created some animals for food to humans; some animals were created for transportation; others animals for our protection, such as Maruca's dog (four-footed canine male mammal), Nero; other animals were created for our entertainment, "pets" like birds and cats; and other animals that God had created were there just to demonstrate God's vast, rich, and diverse power. However, the animals were in second place (2nd) on God's love scale. God's love toward his people would be in the first (1st) place. People were created in "his image"; people had "souls" and God was interested in their "souls." Animals don't have souls. So, for caring, administrating, and controlling the kingdom of the animals, God had given the job to the people, humanity. God had made animals less intelligent than people, and that was why people were obliged to care for and respect animals.

Also, Mercedes had said that now that "domestic animals" were acclimated to the "New World." People in this New World had the privilege and the opportunity of expanding their knowledge of God's creation. Maruca La Chapina's mother knew that large animals could be helpful in transporting people from one place to another, especially to go to work far away from home. Her father would utilize his horse, Arrow, when riding alone. At times, Maruca would accompany her father to ride on a horse (four-footed male equine mammal). Maruca's brother was the one in charge of caring for their horses; he would be in charge of feeding them and keeping then dry and safe inside the barn. He would give them salt to eat, to kill parasites such as fleas and horseflies infesting on this four-footed male equine mammal; and he would brush their horse's hair, mane, and tail.

Maruca's father had a team of oxen (four-footed bovine mammals) that would help him carry/drag the plow in a ground soil that was dry and tough, and because of their help, planting of corn or beans could be done in a shorter time.

Maruca La Chapina's father liked to hunt for food that he would take home as a meal for the whole family; he would hunt for rabbits (rodents and mammals), turkeys (bird, male and female Aves), snakes (reptiles), and wild birds (Aves). Also, Maruca's family enjoyed the companionship of their mascota, Nero (four-footed male canine mammal). Their dog, Nero, would "bark" and "bark" to warn Max and Eugenio, if people or animals would be in proximity of their property. Mainly, Nero would protect their chickens (domestic birds Aves) from foxes, coyotes, and thieves (four-footed mammals).

Maruca La Chapina appreciated the beautiful plumage of the bird called quetzal, the national bird of Guatemala. A male quetzal (ave trogoniform) has a long tail and an elegant breast that is crimson red in color. It is also known as a "paradise" bird. In general, Maruca enjoyed observing all sorts of birds flying around their home in Escuintla, Guatemala. She also appreciated the cleverness of "green parrots" (male and female Aves) from Peten, Guatemala (a mountainous rainforest). She could teach them to imitate many words, commands, and sounds in Spanish.

Maruca La Chapina was thankful to God for being born in a beautiful place like Guatemala, a place with a lot of natural resources such as streams, rivers, mountains, valleys, volcanoes, and lakes and with rainy and dry seasons; and to the west of Escuintla is the great Pacific Ocean. Guatemala also has the ability to grow a variety of fruit and vegetables and the opportunity to care for domestic animals. Maruca knew that all these were blessings from God; Maruca knew how to recognize God's love for her.

CHAPTER 6

The Garden of Eden's Procession

Maruca La Chapina could notice the physical differences between Maximiliano, her brother, and herself. She knew she was younger than Max; she had wavy and longer hair; she liked it when her mother would make "pipe curls" on her hair and tie them up with ribbons, or when she would make her hair a couple of braids. Maruca wore earrings on her ear lobes, and she could see that these would beautifully adorn her face. Maruca La Chapina would dress in long and simple cottony clothes. Maximiliano would help his father with work outdoors. Maruca knew that her brother was braver and gutsier than her; he could grab a fish with his bare hands in the "fish trap" and catch a fowl to be butchered without hesitation. Maruca and Maximiliano knew that they were the only "survivors" of Eugenio and Mercedes' thirteen (13) children, the only ones who outlasted illnesses and diseases from the years the 1920s to 1940s living in Escuintla, Guatemala.

Eugenio's family was known and loved by the people of their town. So when Maruca and Maximiliano were chosen by the church's procession committee to represent characters on a "float," Eugenio and Mercedes were delighted to allow their children to participate in the church's event.

A procession, an evangelism tool in the New World, meant a call to the people from their hideouts at mountains and hills to the valley church to gather for mass and to hear the word of God being preached by the clergy.

The float in the procession was going to be the "Garden of Eden"—the creation of the story in the book of Genesis, the first book in the Bible. Maruca La Chapina was selected to represent Eve, and Maximiliano was selected to represent the devil or Satan, who came to the Garden to tempt Eve. Another child from town was selected to represent the character of Adam, the first man created by God.

Since Eugenio thought of himself as a creative and innovative individual, he challenged his skills by building the platform with the help of other parishioners in the church. However, Eugenio and the building committee were guided by the "padre"—the church's priest—on all details of the float. Eugenio took it personally; after all, his children were going to be in the procession. Maruca was the youngest; she was only five years old. Eugenio wanted the children to be safe on the float while being pulled by horses through the streets of the town. The float had to represent the "Garden of Eden." Animals and greenery (vegetation) were made out of paper, straw, tree leaves, corn husks, and branches. Mercedes worked on the "costumes" for her children; Maruca wore white gown and a white "perraje" that covered her head. Mercedes made a yellow and green costume for Maximiliano, as he represented the serpent in the "Creation" story.

On the day of the procession, the town's church was decorated with fresh flowers (narcises). The unique aroma was sensed as soon as anyone entered the church's threshold. New candles were lit, the floors were clean and polished, and people were congregating in anticipation of the "festivity." Street vendors were preparing their hand-pushcarts carrying food and fruit. Weaved straw baskets were overflowing with candles. Prepared sweets "golosinas" on tables were displayed to salivate people's mouths, besides making the honey bees buzz around. Children were playing and anxious too, especially Maruca and Maximiliano. Eugenio was running around in and out of the church to place more wood and paper around where the children were going to be.

Like any Christian procession done in the country, it was preceded by a member of the clergy carrying the cross, the cross of Jesus Christ with the sign over him, which reading "INRI" meaning "Jesus of Nazareth, the King of the Jews." That was the symbol of the "Old World" (Europe) into the "New World" carried by the Spaniards' discoverers, Christopher Columbus's crew. It meant "civilization" and "salvation" through Jesus Christ.

But Eugenio had additionally erected a cross also with the letters INRI, on the float. The horses were harnessed and waiting patiently to go all groomed with their tails and manes braided and tied in bows done by other parishioners. The church's bells were ringing loudly more than ever. The float was almost done; Eugenio's baby girl looked illuminated and precious. Eugenio had built high benches on the float for the children to sit on. The priest had given special *posing* details for Maruca to do on the float; she had to have her palms together, with her fingertips touching her chin, her head and eyes looking down as showing humility and obedience to God's word. "Congratulations, favored lady! The Lord is with you!" (Luke 1: 28–33).

The float went through the main streets of the town, with a musical band following and playing some praising tunes. People waved and cheered at the children when they passed by. Maximiliano and another other boy smiled and waved back at the spectators. After the musical band, street vendors followed along with other "unbelievers and curious" people, followed lastly by one or two street dogs looking for waste/rubbish from the procession or perhaps looking for a master ("amo") to take them home.

At the end of the procession, everybody, except the dogs, went inside the church for a mass of "repentance and thanksgiving" to God. After the mass outside the church, people continued with the celebration, they purchased food (corn, rice drinks, and corn products with pork meat) from street vendors and had fun with family and friends. Needless to say, the town's "creation" parade was a "success," and thanks to God, there were no incidents or accidents, while Maximiliano and Maruca were going on the float. Eugenio and Mercedes's family were given thanks by the priest for demonstrating their faith, obedience, and dedication to the Word of God.

CHAPTER 7

Choosing a Mango from a Tree

Maruca La Chapina knew that besides the variety of animals in her world, there was also a variety of fruits, vegetables, and flowers that she enjoyed eating. Among the vegetables that Maruca loved to find at the market at a good price were beets, "pacayas," "yucas," carrots, potatoes, green beans, and peas. Among the "edible" flowers were palo de izote and the "flor de pito." Among the spicy condiments were the commonly called chiles; Maruca La Chapina's favorite without doubt were the "chiltepes." They were small, but they were intensely "hot." Among the fruits that Maruca La Chapina loved to eat were "pitayas," "anonas," pineapples, granadillas, granadas, nísperos, chicos, zapotes, bananas, oranges, and coconuts.

But to Maruca La Chapina, there was no other fruit that tickles her taste buds as mango does; Maruca enjoyed eating mangos of every kind, color, and shape found nearby the Pacific Ocean. In Guatemala, there were green mangos, there were juicy mangos, there were yellow mangos, there were orange mangos, there were fleshy mangos, and there were stringy mangoes.

One time when Maruca's family was visiting a farm at Gonzalo's place, at the northeast of Escuintla, Guatemala, in the Departamento of Jalapa, Maruca experienced several adventures with God's creation—animals, plants, and her. Gonzalo decided right away to take the family—everyone—for a walk and see the gardens, fruit trees, and animals. Maruca La Chapina's family enjoyed this experience very much when they had the opportunity.

This time the analytical Maruca noticed that among the trees growing at the "farm," there was a mango tree that had ripe mangoes. Maruca was thrilled by her discovery because no one had mentioned it to her, when everyone (family and friends) was walking, admiring the different vegetation, flora, and soil from another part of her country of Guatemala. Then, after the walk, all went back to have refreshments at the house's front "veranda/porch." Maruca however had decided to go back on her own and take a second look at the mango tree she spotted; after all, Maruca La Chapina loved mangoes like no one else.

She recognized the trunk of the tree, the leaves on the tree were uniquely elongated and sparkled, and most surely the shape of its tempting fruit. She happily concluded that the mango fruit was also growing in the south of the country.

Maruca La Chapina decided to take the opportunity and taste a mango from an area with different types of soil that was a lighter color and less fertile than the soil found in Escuintla. However, at the same time, she thought she was overstepping her boundaries and trust from the family's friends by walking on her own at the farm. She had been educated at home by her parents—about the virtues—a conformity to a standard. But she decided to do it anyway. Luckily, the mango tree was not that far from the main home.

Once Maruca got to the location of the mango tree, she contemplated which mango to hit and pull off with a stick that she had found near the tree. Then, while searching for the best-looking mango on the tree, she saw a delicious-looking mango that she thought she could reach with her stick. She simultaneously wished to get help from "gravity," the earth's gravitational force. The ripe mango could just have fallen right there without hers or any other human effort, just as in the story of Isaac Newton's falling green apple. But no one was there to help her.

In reality, Maruca thought this piece of fruit was not just "a common green apple," as the apples you could find on the ground at an apple's orchard. This mango was still connected through its stem on the tree. Mangoes required an applied and specific force to pull them down from the tree. The stems on the mango trees were thicker than apple trees.

In the meantime, while Maruca was looking up at the mango tree's branches, she hadn't noticed that when she was trying to stand at the highest point of the ground near the tree, to give her a vertical "boost," she was standing at the peak of an "ant hill." The red and black ants' reaction was that, of course, after being invaded and trampled, they started attacking Maruca. The alarmed and violent ants ran up Maruca's sandaled feet and bare legs and the ants started biting her. So Maruca's reaction was to run away from the mango tree and the ant hill as fast as she could. She was screaming for help and at the same time, she was removing her fastened sandals from her feet and killing the ants that were still running down her feet and legs. Fortunately, Maruca's mom, dad, and family friends heard her screaming and rushed to help her, to give first aid for the ant bites on her feet and legs.

In the end, Maruca did not remove the fruit from the mango tree, but since the family, friends, and farm owners appreciated the visit and felt sympathetic for Maruca's bad experience with the ants, they got a ripped and sweet mango from the tree, peeled, sliced, and offered it to her on a "platter" for her enjoyment.

The lesson this time for Maruca was that besides feeling obligated to express her "pardon" to her family and friends for her self-reliance, she should ask her parents or family friends for some mango slices to taste—mangos from another region within the country of Guatemala.

Most likely they would have gladly given her some mangos without hesitation. But Maruca wanted to taste a mango from a tree, a mango spotted by her, and pulled it off from the tree through her own effort. Well, the trip to the east of Escuintla, Guatemala, had an educational learning lesson for Maruca La Chapina. Maruca's lesson was that insects—bugs (invertebrates with six legs) such as ants—who live in colonies enjoyed mangos as well as her. In addition, Maruca learned that insects living in trees should not be ignored by humans.

However, Gonzalo made it known to Maruca's family that, on the contrary, he had invited Maruca's family to visit his farm;

the farm was open to each member of the family, and he felt ultimately responsible for those mean ants living under the mango tree.
Unfortunately, it was an underestimation on his part. He regretted
the inconvenience to Maruca La Chapina. Maruca La Chapina knew
about God's creation not living harmonically always. She knew per
the Bible, God had assigned humans/people to be the "steward."

But that was not all for experiences at Gonzalo's farm.

She had the opportunity to observe closely an arachnid (invertebrate with eight legs)—a "tarantula" running in the middle of the
patio, but visible in the moonlight—while she was playing with
other girls the game called jump rope. A brave and bold young man
at the farm stopped the spider and grabbed it with a rag in his hands
to show the children visiting the farm.

By then, everyone had stopped in their tracks, admiring the
symmetrical, intricate, and so perfect parts of the "giant spider"—its
hairy legs and body, its multiple eyes, and its two markable body
parts. Maruca, of course, didn't have anything to say, so she just let the
"young man" from the farm impress everybody with his understanding and knowledge of arachnids—another God's small creatures.

All the children were silence, observing from afar, and enter-
tained with some kind of reverent "awe," then the tarantula was
released on the ground. The "young man" from the farm said tarantulas were common in the area because he had seen them around
the stables where the farmer was breeding horses. The "young man"
from the farm said that tarantulas were not "toys." They also were not
poisonous but did have a painful bite. Most of all, tarantulas did not
give the impression of any benefits by living close to humans.

Surprisingly, when the children were exchanging comments
on other small creatures such as insects, the conversation changed
to riding horses; this subject gave a "stroke of wonder" to Maruca's
mind with the idea of riding horses on unfamiliar territory. Then she
asked the adults if they could ride horses the following day. Gonzalo
granted Maruca's wishes. Maruca's trip to a farm located northeast of
Escuintla was getting to be very adventurous.

The next day after breakfast, the children, visitors, and some
adults went to the stables, where horses were being saddled and bri-

dled to go horseback riding. When Maruca La Chapina was helped to mount a horse, she didn't know what kind of horse she was going to get. She knew that some horses (cuadrúpedo hoofed mammal equine) could be very temperamental. Maruca was mounted on a "pardo"—a brown-colored horse with white spots on both sides.

Maruca very soon found out the horse she was riding on was "ornery," and its name was Capricho. The horse did not want to be steered by her. Maruca wanted to follow the riders ahead of her because she was unfamiliar with the territory. The "young man" of the farm with the name of Matias had instructed everyone to ride together, so no one would become lost. But Maruca's horse went its own way and stopped by a tree, to munch, on its small and yellow leaves. Maruca directed the horse's reins with force to follow the other riders, to move away from the tree, and kicked her heels against the horse's sides, as it was explained to her by Matias. Maruca saw the horse's irritable disposition, then she just smiled, laughed, and allowed the horse to take a break. Then she thought the horse wanted to munch, before going for a ride.

Matias, the young man from the farm who was in charge of guiding the cavalcade (other riders), noticed Maruca's horse, Capricho, was not following the other riders. Then Matias, firmly and loudly, called the horse by its name, Capricho, and gave a lash to Capricho's posterior muscles (gluteus). Then Maruca's horse jolted, stopped munching, and started following the riders ahead of them. Maruca La Chapina thought that "discipline" was not only gratifying for people, but the people could benefit from animals that were disciplined.

The horseback riding was entertaining and interesting. The cavalcade went through roads with big rocks; the vegetation of the region was typical of an arid region consisting of thorny bushes, cactus, and low elevations. The horse, Capricho, was obedient the rest of the way. Matias apologized to Maruca for Capricho's behavior at the beginning of their ride and said that Capricho was well-fed before the ride (hay, straw, and oats). So the horse shouldn't have been hungry. Probably, Capricho was testing Maruca's horsemanship. So Matias added that Capricho's name was well-suited for their "pardo" horse.

Also at the farm, Maruca was able to observe the making of dairy products made out of cow's milk such as cheese and butter. She especially enjoyed drinking milk straight from the cow's udder. The trip to the farm concluded with a luncheon of "friendship and celebration" with a meal of "fried pork" with güisquiles and potatoes, black beans, and of course fresh, handmade tortillas, coffee, and fresh milk.

CHAPTER 8

Following a Trail

Maruca La Chapin loved to eat chicken eggs (poultry), and living in Escuintla, Guatemala, she had the opportunity to taste not just hen eggs, but she also had tasted turtle's eggs, iguana eggs, caiman eggs, snake eggs, turkey eggs, duck eggs, goose eggs, and also fish's eggs. Maruca La Chapina knew that with a pair or few chicken eggs, she could scramble them and add any spice, herb, and vegetable or any kind of meat and end up with an exquisite food dish for the entire family. Therefore, chicken eggs were a very important "food item" in Maruca La Chapina's family food diet. Even though the hens that laid eggs that were living in the family's chicken coop were few, they were very nourished and cared for because the entire family depended on them.

Maruca La Chapina expected several times a week that she would be able to gather eggs laid by their hens; to Maruca, it was "a guessing game" to find eggs among the boxes, the straw, food/water buckets, tree branches, and bleachers in the chicken coop inside the barn ("el granero") building. But every year was more interesting for Maruca when her mom, Mercedes, would choose which "chick" to separate from the rest and to lay eggs in the chicken coop. Moreover, Maruca's mom would prefer to buy at the market hen chicks with colored feathers such as gray feathers, yellow feathers, black feathers, brown feathers, and orange feathers, but not "hen chicks" with white feathers.

Mercedes believed that "colored feathers" poultry were more flavorful than "white-feathered" poultry, and she was passing this information to Maruca. Maruca La Chapina would enjoy counting the eggs on the nest from a "broody" hen then observe the day that she would remain on her nest and away from the other chickens, and then after approximately twenty-one days of incubation, Maruca would count the number of eggs hatched into little chicks. Every now and then, especially when Nero was a puppy ("cachorrito"), the family would lose an egg, a chick, or a chicken to a "thief predator." So Nero needed some training to become the best hunting dog. Eugenio, Max, and their dog, Nero, would go in pursuit on their trail to prevent another robbery. They followed tracks of wild animals such as foxes, ocelots, opossums, and raccoons.

Maruca La Chapina remembered the time when Eugenio and Max had to get out of bed in the middle of the night to follow a trail of an intruder. Nero was anxiously, furiously, and constantly barking. Something was not right; something had happened at their property or somebody was hidden. Usually at night, "Nero" would let loose in the yard of the property. Their dog would look forward to this part of the day because he liked to run freely on the entire property, especially at the barn where grain and the animals were kept.

Nero was a happy dog; Mercedes thought that Nero liked his job as a "guardian" dog. But that night, Nero was fixing his eyes beyond the property and kept on barking. Eugenio thought that perhaps a raccoon or taquasin had entered and was able to break into the barn (granero). Maybe Nero had decided to take a nap on the wooden bench on the cushion, by the big door, that night, and someone had broken through the fence behind the barn and robbed the chicken coop. So Eugenio decided to go and find out what was outside their back fence that didn't settle right with Nero. Then Eugenio went to look for his rifle, and Max went to get his "club."

There was nothing Mercedes and Maruca could do, so they went back to bed to wait for their men's news and their dog, Nero. They walked toward the fence's portion northeast and noticed the fence's gate was unfasted. Their animals could go through this fence while it was wide open to grace. This filled their minds with doubt that they were dealing with a common animal as a "raccoon" (an omnivorous and nocturnal mammal) or an opossum (an omnivorous, marsupial, nocturnal mammal). Then, outside their fence, Nero took the lead to show the way to Eugenio and Max, and Nero quit barking and started sniffing. Eugenio and Max were relying on their hearing for rustling noises. The night was clear and calm with the help of a full moon. They had walked as far as two hundred meters when they got to a dense vegetation of a small ravine with trees when they heard a dragging noise of someone on the ground.

Nero started to bark again; Eugenio and Max prepared and aimed their weapons at where the noise was coming from. Then they saw a man who appeared to be wounded, unarmed, and inappropriately clothed, scruffy, for cold night conditions. Eugenio, who was annoyed by the whole ordeal, started asking questions to the "intruder" on the ground, and the "intruder" frighteningly responded to Eugenio without taking his eyes off Nero. The "intruder" told Eugenio that he was on his way to look for work south of the area and that he hadn't had a bite to eat in days, nor money to buy food. But when he was passing by Eugenio's property, the intruder heard the crow from Eugenio's rooster. So the intruder also thought that might have been at that location, a chicken coop with hens and eggs—eggs to eat. Then the "intruder" said that he unlatched the gate and walked into the property—Eugenio's property—but he didn't even make it to the chicken coop because the dog stopped him and bit his hands, when he was trying to defend himself from him.

Then at that time the only option the "intruder" had was to run and jump over the fence and get out of the property. However, the strap of one of his sandals caught the fence post, spraining his ankle and making him fall to the ground and dragging his leg across a sharp nail, which left a deep cut on his leg.

After listening to the man's sad story, Eugenio and Max felt compassion and pity for the "intruder." By now, he had revealed his name to Eugenio. His name was Cayetano Xelaju. Then Eugenio forgave his misdeed and decided to help him instead by sending Max and their dog back home to get their horse named Slingshot and some blankets. In the meantime, Eugenio and Cayetano talked more about the incident.

Once at home, Eugenio prepared a resting place—a straw mattress—for Cayetano at their barn to sleep. In addition, Nero was tied up again to help everyone have a good night's rest and prevent him from biting Cayetano again. The next day, Eugenio cleaned and cared for Cayetano's wounds, Mercedes prepared a good breakfast for Cayetano with some extra tortillas, and as a surprise, Eugenio designed and made "wooden crutches" to help Cayetano get faster to his destination.

At the end of the day, Maruca's family expressed affection for their pet "Nero," by petting his "head and back." In addition, Mercedes made a soup ("caldo") for Nero, from a "ham" bone with lots of tortillas and additional salt—Nero's favorite meal. Maruca and Max were proud of their pet for being brave and loyal. The following day, Eugenio and Max had to repair their fence by nailing the loose wooden planks.

CHAPTER 9

The Beach

When there was opportunity to go near a famous beach at Guatemala's seashore line, the "San Jose's port" was Maruca La Chapina's favorite one to visit with her family. At San Jose's port, the temperature and humidity were greater than at home in Escuintla. The *temperature average was between 60 and 105 degrees Fahrenheit.*

Maruca La Chapina could see the spume/foam forming on the sea waves that would go up and down on the black (volcanic) sand beach. Also, she could hear the quick harmonious sound between the different seawater currents. At noon, the family would look for the shade of a "hut" on the beach, while quenching their thirst with the semisweet juice of recently harvested coconuts. In the background, the sound coming from "cicadas" (invertebrate insects) could also be heard, playing their inspired "chorale songs" of heat and humidity with their back legs.

Maruca La Chapina knew that at San Jose's port, the family could walk over the black sand for miles along the seaside and pick up wherever the evening's tide had thrown on the beach such as sea-shells and skeletons of animals. Maruca and Max could also chase the small crabs appearing and disappearing between the sand and waves. But one day while the family was walking during the first hours of the day, they found the carcass of a "puffer fish" fully inflated. It looked like a small balloon, shaped like a fish with spikes. Max said that probably the fish had lived its entire fish's life because no animal or people could eat them. The meat of a puffer fish is very poisonous. Among other significant observations of being at the beach for Maruca was the spotting of "bird swallows" (migratory aves) called Golondrinas. Maruca liked the way the Golondrinas swayed over the surf early in the evenings; they appeared as almost kissing the salty water, while making a cry of happiness as their long wings were getting sprinkled with water.

Going to the beach of San Jose's, looking at the immensity of the Pacific Ocean at the sunsets, with a "great orange"—the sun—and sitting on a horizontal line made Maruca La Chapina's family felt grateful, undeserving, and amazed of God's creation wonders, power, and love. Surely the visits at the sea were not completed until the family savored the goodness of "seafood," either "bacalao/cod" or "atún/tuna," fried or wrapped in egg with tomato sauce, or "seafood" soup with lots of vegetables, shrimp, and other mollusks. Plus the usual side dishes, such as beet and cauliflower salads, tortillas, of course, and perhaps accompanied with black beans and rice too. At the end of her meal, Maruca La Chapina had the opportunity once again to thank God through thanking her parents by providing her with "delicious food," while visiting "El Puerto de San Jose" in Guatemala.

CHAPTER 10

Jesus, the Spiritual Light of the Universe

Maruca La Chapina understood that her home was near the Pacific Ocean and that the country of Guatemala had an ocean called Atlantic to the northeast, in which Eugenio, her father, had said that it was "far away" from home. He would say that would take him many, many days on "horseback" to get to that location.

But one Sunday at the plaza, after mass, a family from town stayed talking to Maruca's family (her father and brother). Maruca listened to the conversation about Saint Christopher and the plans the town was making for the annual celebration. Nowadays the festivity is known as "El dia de la raza" (the Human race)—"Columbus Day"—crossing the Atlantic. But Maruca La Chapina had heard more about this name. The "padre" at the church had said that Saint Christopher had brought "Jesus Christ" on his shoulders to the "New World"; he had crossed the ocean, the "Atlantic Ocean" that is. He explored the world by "sailing ships" and with the help and direction of God the Father.

History is supported by adding the following: Lake Izabal is located in the northeast of the country of Guatemala; the name was given after the name of the Catholic "Queen of Spain." In those days in Europe, around the year of 1492, people believed planet Earth had the geometrical shape of a four-side "table," just a "flat surface with four coordinates (N, S, W, and E)"—Europe being at the center of that table. This was because when "nervy and bold" people could and would venture on ships and go beyond the "disappearing" lines—meaning, in the human eyes, the horizon—many of them would never return to the point of departure and maybe it was because of shipwrecks, pirates, bad storms, lack of wind, and etc. So, when Columbus, decided to go and find out for himself, he found himself lacking "finances" and "power."

After going to the political "superpowers of the day" for help, no one believed otherwise and did not want to help him on his voyages. The Catholic queen of Spain, Isabella (not her husband), the Catholic queen representing the country of Spain, decided to "finance" Columbus's voyages. However, her being a "devoted Catholic," the queen requested evangelization of humans found in the New World, if he found any on his voyages, with the help of "clergymen." Furthermore, the symbol of the cross of "Jesus Christ" had to be taken on all ships and the cross had to be erected at the "new lands," if he found any. Fortunately, Christopher Columbus found a "New World," and soon, the news was brought back to the queen of Spain and to the rest of Europe.

Back to Maruca's conversation outside their church, Maruca also heard the other family talk about "Castillo de San Felipe" named after the queen's husband. San Felipe's castle (1500s) was a "fortress" with long walls of stones and mortar, built to protect the country and in fact, during those days, the entire continent. It was built to protect them from pirates from France, Portugal, and England, including moors from Africa. They also talked about a river called Rio Dulce that was a large river, full of reptiles such as alligators and crocodiles. The river's water was not salty, and its water would flow into the country of Honduras and Caribbean Seas.

Maruca was content to live near the Pacific Ocean and volcanoes. The volcanoes were Pacaya, Agua, Fuego, and Santiaguito. But the most spectacular part of this reality was that on some occasions, Maruca and Mercedes would have the opportunity to observe some volcanic activity. First, they said, just before the volcano eruption, a rumbling noise from the ground was emitted, and there was a sound like animals running—a stampede. Maruca and her brother would step outside the house and look for the "red cloud" in the sky. It could be observed the eruptions of "red lava" run down the volcano. The following day "volcanic ash" was observed covering the ground and on the washing tubs of the town; and the sky was overcast for days.

About the earthquakes, there were no definite warnings. Maruca's observations on earthquakes were that they happened at night when planet Earth cooled off. People in the area knew that they didn't have to build their houses near the volcano's cone sides, especially if the volcano was known to be "active" in the last few years. Earthquakes made noises underneath the ground and the ground moved in all directions. If people were caught being outdoors, they could lose their footing, break a bone, or fall to the ground. If people were caught indoors during an earthquake, the house's roof could fall on the people.

Maruca La Chapina's family had experienced a number of these phenomenal geological events (earthquakes and volcanic eruptions), living in Escuintla, Guatemala. But, thanks to God, the family (Eugenio, Mercedes, Max, and Maruca), was able to "get out of the house on time" to find refuge under the door's frames and to "tell about it" later. Because Maruca and Mercedes knew that God was always with them.

When Maruca's family came back from church, Mercedes was happy and excited about a purchase she had made that day. She had bought a photograph of the painting of "el niño de atoche" (an icon) and that it had been blessed by the church's priest. Then she started to tell the story about the painting. It was the painting of the King Jesus called niño de atoche, but maybe just as other words in the Spanish language, the word *atoche* had lost its correct pronunciation but not its meaning. The meaning was that the "God-child" was the one who brings light/fuego/torch—"the light of the world."

The history behind the "picture" was that the "original artist" with the idea from the country of "Spain," the old world, had made the image of the child Jesus. The child had a crown on his head and a scepter in his hand; however, other people believed that it was a "wooden cross" in his hands. He also was wearing a "royal cloak" made out of velvet. The idea was taken to the country of Guatemala, and from many years back, it was known as a picture frame of the "el niño con la antorcha." This picture represented Mercedes as a "personal investment" for a great cause; she would always have this painting with her wherever she relocated because the picture was a good theme of conversation for the people who saw it. She liked to tell about the child Jesus who had brought light to a dark world; the name of that child was and is "Jesus Christ" the only son of God— the only way to God the Father.

CHAPTER 11

Day of Rest

Maruca La Chapina was always mesmerized by God's creation: the vegetation/plants, great and small animals, and people. Maruca La Chapina had even created and learned "sign language" with hands; she communicated with her family through this.

When she referred to people, her sign language was the sign of the "cruz" made by the church's "padre" (father, son, and the holy ghost), a sign used at the end of "confession" and at the end of the mass. When she would refer to animals, the hand sign would be as if she was going to shake her hands with someone. When she would refer to plants, the hand sign would be as if she was getting a "manicure."

People could intervene with animals and plants to improve their relationship of gains and benefits for everyone, as God had called us to do in the book of Genesis of the Bible. In her observations, Maruca knew that animals showed love and responsibility to their "young." For example, in order to protect their pigeons (aves) from predators, Maruca's father had built an elevated (four or five feet off the ground) pigeon coup out of wood. Maruca's family would eat pigeons because they tasted good, and they were quite nutritious, especially when Mercedes, Maruca's mom, would prepare them fried among sliced onions in tomato sauce with carrots or other vegetables, surrounded with rice or fried potatoes.

The mother and father pigeons would collect and carry food to their nests; they would also take turns at night to keep watch over their nest. Maruca La Chapina knew that her parents loved and cared for her when they would make meals and bring home food to eat made by her mother, when they would buy clothing to cover and protect her body, and when they would take her to church to learn about God the Creator of the world and God the Savior of humanity.

Maruca's parents would also talk to her about being busy working with her hands to keep her out of trouble, besides it was pleasing to God and her parents. Furthermore, Maruca learned about commerce (free trade), when she was taken to the market to negotiate prices with vendors about animals, vegetables, fruits, already prepared food, and articles of clothing.

The land that God had given to Guatemalans was good; the soil received plenty of solar energy and plenty of nutrients during rainy seasons, and with some "sweaty hard work," it was possible to have a "bumper" crop of vegetables and fruits from a variety of plants. Perhaps Maruca La Chapina did not know that "God the Creator" had given third place to planet Earth in the solar system. Perhaps Maruca had not heard about the definitions of the words *latitude*, *equator*, *longitude*, and *poles*, which are imaginary lines of the globe/sphere-shaped planet. But actually, she was appreciative of the distance between where she lived in Escuintla, Guatemala, and the sun. Because she knew she wasn't far from the sun to make her shiver and get goosebumps, and she wasn't too close to the sun to make her flare up in spontaneous flames (Genesis 1:16–18).

Another good example was when Maruca's brother, Maximiliano, worked with his father, Eugenio, at a carpentry room building "fish traps" to catch fish at the creeks and streams of water near their home. At times he'd catch enough to sell fish to friends and neighbors. Maruca's family would enjoy eating freshwater fish, but they were not easy to catch. Maruca was grateful when Maximiliano would bring fish home to eat. Maruca thought that the ability to catch fish required some kind of skill and nerve, especially when fish were taken out of the "fish trap"; fish were slippery and jumpy and had sharp fins that cut and hurt your hands.

Among Maruca's favorite fish from freshwater were bluegills with teeth and catfish (juilín). Las "mojarras" were fried, and "catfish" was cut up into chunks and put into soup with vegetables plus other types of seafood. One Sunday, a day of rest, Maruca's family took a trip to fish, to have an outdoor lunch, and to enjoy the panoramic view of the higher elevation, the entrance to a national "park" with a road between tall trees at the mountains of Chimaltenango Departamento—a cooler area called Los Aposentos Park.

Maximiliano was always enthusiastic about trying out his work spent on making a "fish trap" with his father. The fish trap was placed at the bottom, under the lake's edge vegetation, and at a narrow side of the lake; small shrimp were used for bait.

While Max and his father watched and waited for a fish to enter the "fish trap," Maruca and her mother decided to walk around the lake. Maruca knew that at times, the birds called swans could be found swimming around the lake; it was eye-opening to observe these types of big birds covered with white feathers, swimming gracefully on the water with their long feathered necks. Once in a while, it was more fun to find a mother swan swimming with one or two "chicks" on her back. The mother swan was most careful when walking on the ground with her young. Moreover, both of the parent swans could be a little violent to humans, raising their wings, when protecting their young.

This time Maruca noticed that there were swans on the lake, but they didn't have young ones with them, and they were far away from the lake's edge to have a close look. So Maruca and her mother walked back to the point where they thought the "fish trap" was left and placed.

Seeing that Eugenio and Max were not waiting for them at the location, Maruca decided to check the fish trap for herself. She understood that the side of the lake where the "fish trap" was placed was not very deep, so she spotted some large stones where to place her feet for "dry" footing and for a better view of the fish trap. But Maruca didn't know that a "tiny" plant called moss could grow on rocks near the water, another part of God's creation. Then at the moment Maruca placed her feet on the rock, Maruca slipped and fell into the water. Maruca ended up wet and surprised, and with

Mercedes's help Maruca was able to get out of the water and forgot completely about checking the "fish trap."

When Eugenio and Max came back from their walk, they retrieved the "fish trap" from the lake that was without bait and without large fish to eat, practically empty. In the "fish trap," there were just two (2) "tiny fish" that were too small to eat. When Max retrieved the trap from the water, the fish got out. Then Max decided to give the fish trap another chance. Max rebaited his fish trap and placed the box at another location in the lake.

Meanwhile, while they waited, Mercedes unpacked her lunch basket and served lunch to her family: Guatemalan style "chiles rellenos," large peppers stuffed with pork meat and vegetables, wrapped in an egg inside a bread bun. Also, Mercedes served "plantain dough" stuffed with pureed sweetened black beans. For drinks, she served them "warm" juice made from crushed sweet corn.

Max waited and when he checked the box again. He said out loud, "Tepocates!" ("Tadpoles!) Then Maruca exclaimed, "What are you saying, Max?"

"He said 'tadpoles.'" Maruca had never heard this word mentioned, which was a small animal swimming in the water with tail and fins. Tadpoles did not have their bodies covered with scales, their exterior cover appeared smooth and black in color. Max told Maruca that these kinds of animals were "young" frogs and toads. Amphibians are animals adapted to live in water and land (young vertebrates between fishes and reptiles). Max added that some of the stone paintings and sculptures of the Mayan Quiché cultures included these types of animals because they were fascinated by them. Also, Max told Maruca that one of the things he appreciated about going to school was that he was learning all other kinds of words not commonly used at home, and he was glad to share information with his sister at home.

Eugenio's family knew that fishing had many variables. Max thought that his "fish trap" could use new improvements and told himself that the next time was going to be better. But the most important thing was that the family had had a good time, enjoying the good temperature and having a family lunch outdoors under tall trees and the mountains of Chimaltenango, Guatemala, where more clothing was required to cover the body, such as wool fibers and not cotton fibers in the form of jackets, blankets, sweaters, ponchos, etc.

Meanwhile, Max and Maruca were enhancing their knowledge of God's animal kingdom. Then, when Eugenio was preparing the wagon to head back home, they observed a "flock of goats," ringing their bells, and under the care of their shepherd, offering milk to drink. Max and Maruca asked if they could get goat's milk. Mercedes permitted their children to drink creamy and warm milk from goats before their trip back home. Mercedes knew that the warm milk was going to help her children to calm down and take a nap. After all, everybody had had good days in the cold mountains in Guatemala.

Father Abraham…has many sons…mmmm…
many sons…mmmmm… Father Abraham…
I nonetheless… Father Abraham…has many daughters too…
mmmm… Father Abraham…has many daughters too! Amen.

CHAPTER 12

Patience

Maruca La Chapina knew that the virtue of patience was good to practice because it would yield great rewards; she knew that many events that happened around her were out of her control. However, Maruca also knew that she could influence the ultimate results of other events. Maruca knew that the factor of "time" was an important component for animals to grow their young ones. In other words, they needed "incubation time," from eggs to chickens, from eggs to pigeons, and from eggs to turkeys. The corn stalks took "growing time" to get their ears of corn full of "juicy plump" kernels. It took time to drain the "sap" from the "rubber" trees, in the forest near the Pacific Ocean. This sap was collected in buckets tied to the tree's trunks, which were sold to companies making rubber.

Also, many types of invertebrates—insects "larvae" such as caterpillars—go through their metamorphosis. Many of these caterpillars looked very colorful and dramatic with their spikes and spots. This was because many of them are poisonous to birds and other predators. Maruca La Chapina very well knew not to touch them and only observe them from afar to do their God-mandated job. These caterpillars could eat the entire bush's leaves, so they spun themselves in a web—a cocoon—to go to sleep. Then later these would look like "dormant white pills" that would open to release the insects called butterflies or moths. Now they didn't look like spiky caterpillars, but they were "butterflies" that would extend their wings and fly away as beautiful curious creatures sitting on bouganville flowers and the orange blossoms of orange trees.

Maruca La Chapina's favorite butterflies were the ones with turquoise-blue wings. Also, among the other animals that Maruca La Chapina liked to observe on their patio at home were the "snails"; they appeared to be like a "small worm carrying a cute hard shell." These delicate and slow-paced animals took their time, slithering through the "flor del paraíso" stalks.

Maruca La Chapina loved to work along with her mother, cultivating "fertilizer" from "organic waste" of primary fruit and vegetable peelings and rinds. Among the fruits considered to make good fertilizer were coconuts, watermelons, cantaloupe, bananas, papayas, and especially pineapples. Among vegetables, she would use beets. Mercedes's organic fertilizer required plenty of time and work; the "human" work consisted of weekly switching the layers of dirt and waste with a shovel. The "small animals" called bacteria had the bigger job portion of daily work (night and day); they had to transform the large pieces of organic waste into fine, rich in nutrients, black dirt that could be sold at the market.

When Mercedes, Maruca's mom, would decide to make a sour liquid drink called vinegar or cider, of fruit's peelings and rinds, she would put her fruit waste in a closed and sealed clay jar. Then she would give time for "fermentation" to take place and change the flavor. Then sometimes Maruca's mom would add a sugar product to the mixture to alter the acidity of the vinegar. This liquid called vinegar was good to add to salads and meat to bring out the flavor of the food dish.

When preparing good food, Maruca La Chapina would choose to make them in "clay containers" rather than other types of pottery. She had different sizes of dishes and just as the many variables of volume (volume) and N (particles or moles in a gas) could reach infinite values of flavors because they could have differences in their chemistry and with time and patience. Maruca could have had different results every time. However, Maruca was glad to know that God was constant in his love for her. And for example, the constant k was unchangeable, just like God to his people. An example is the formula "constant fundamental of physics" called Avogadro's law: N = k/V where k is = 6.02×10^{23} (never changes).

Among the annual events that Maruca La Chapina earnestly waited to celebrate were Christmas, Easter week, New Years, and her birthday celebration. She knew that birthdays at Eugenio Vasquez's family were special events during the year; the celebration would start in the morning with salutations, hugs, kisses, blessings, and giving thanks to God for another year. Birthdays were noted for eating more than usual of the preferred food tastes. Also, birthdays were good occasions to receive "surprises" such as a brand-new dress, a new pair of sandals/shoes, a slipper, a "madrileña" (head covering), a new coat, or a box of candy, or simply a "vase of freshly picked wildflowers." There would also be a special mass of thanksgiving.

Also, there was time to recognize and follow the famous "Mayan Quiché" tribe tradition of drinking chocolate—a cup of chocolate drink with a pure kosher small wheat cake with aromatic seeds called anise spread with butter. All these awaited at the dining room table, which was dressed with a long and clean "tablecloth."

For lunch or dinner, there were also good "food dishes." Maruca's favorite food dish would include chicken in "gravy" called jocon verde, turkey in gravy called pepian, or a "barbecue" of several kinds of meats with "Mayan sauce" called chirmol with the hot peppers called chiltepes, and of course handmade thick tortillas with cold drink like called horchata and ground rice water with cinnamon and vanilla.

Tamales are very significant in the culture of the country and can be enjoyed at any type of celebration or party. The tamale dish represents a celebration of the two cultures involved in the mixture: Native American tribes and Spanish Europeans. The grain mostly used to make the dough part (besides shortening) is corn, but it can be done as well by using rice. The delicious gravy or sauce that goes in between is made out of a "puree" of ground vegetables such as roasted tomatoes, peppers, and onions. The spices can be salt, fricassee, and sesame seeds. The meat mostly used is pork, but it can be replaced with poultry (chicken or turkey). The wrapping and tying of food materials can be done with the use of banana, corn, and other tropical plant leaves. Finally, don't forget to steam them in a clay pot.

Now, for dessert, she would expect a bowl of fruit such as juicy "jocotes" and/or "nances in honey" and/or "mangos in honey." At the end of her "birthday" celebration, Maruca knew that she had had a "special birthday celebration," and the following day was going to be just another "regular" day of the year. Above all, she had to wait for 365 days to have another unforgettable "special birthday celebration."

CHAPTER 13

National Treasures

Tikal—the Jaguar Temple
Central Park—the National Fountain

After the family lost Eugenio around the 1940s, Mercedes, Maximiliano, and Maruca sold their home in Escuintla and moved to live in the country's capital, Guatemala City. The "valley" where the second capital of Guatemala was founded was called El Valle de la Ermita. The family moved to a completely different environment, a city environment. People's households were built within walking distance, and domestic animals were not easily seen. The markets were plenty and well-diversified. Anyone could acquire any type of food items such as fruits, vegetables, clothing, furniture, and other home articles.

Mercedes was resigned for a new beginning without Eugenio and eager to establish a new home for her and her fatherless adult children. Maruca had found work at a home of the Garcia-Sandoval family near Guatemala's national central park. She worked as a cook for a family who immediately fell in love with her tenacious ways and ability for preparing meals. Maximiliano had found working as a carpenter at the beginning, but eventually, he embraced the idea with the freedom of opening his own carpentry shop in the city. Mercedes enjoyed being at their home with her hardworking children, but soon Maruca's employer requested for her to move into their home with the promise of Maruca having her own living quarters at their home, enough for her mother to move in with her. In addition, Maruca appreciated the idea of saving money to expand their wardrobe and visit the stores at the "Portal del Commercio."

Guatemala's city climate was much cooler than Escuintla. They also needed sturdier comfortable shoes to walk on the paved roads and concrete sidewalks and also additional support for Mercedes's feet, including a pair of nylon stockings for Maruca's legs, one of the latest fashions of the times, with a seam on the back of the legs. Maruca also wanted to buy hats to wear, especially on Sundays.

Maximiliano moved Mercedes's property into his carpentry shop at Guatemala's capital city with the agreement of the family.

The Vasquez-Zelada family surely enjoyed the cooler temperatures in the city and along with the cleanness of walking the streets without stepping on horse droppings. This was because of the advent of the automobile. They also enjoyed the business and street lights around the public park in the central square of the city. The rest of the city streets run east and west or north and south extending out to the rest of the city.

Palm Sunday was a special day for Maruca's family, a day of no work for Maruca and Max, a day to enjoy time with their mother. In the morning, the family celebrated and worshiped together to commemorate the beginning of the Holy Week—precisely *Jesus's victorious entrance to Jerusalem*—by attending mass at the capital's cathedral. A procession was scheduled following the mass. They watched the procession. The church-faith keepers of the committee in charge of the procession had ensured that the wooden colt appeared shiny and without storage marks, as per the Bible (Luke 19:30), a colt without use (young, mammal, four-legged, herbivorous). It was covered with new layers of paint and varnish. The wooden platform carried the image of Jesus on the colt, standing on a thick carpet made of branches of "palm trees" (John 12:14–15).

Then, further, on the platform there were three crosses, the one in the middle with the sign in the Latin language that read "INRI," and a white linen cloth (manto blanco) was displayed.

This was a good visual aid and a reminder to the people of what was expected to come on *Resurrection Sunday* (Mark 16: 5–6).

Then the three of them went home for lunch and rest. In the afternoon, Mercedes and Maruca had gone back to the central park to walk and admired the remarkable beauty of the national architecture of the "plaza" in Guatemala city. This was considered a "national treasure." But these buildings were an addition to the "grandiose" "Mayan cities" that were located throughout the entire country and that had been built many, many years before, such as the Jaguar Temple also known as Tikal. After all, the country of Guatemala was worldly known as being "the cradle of the Mayan tribe."

Central park's plaza could offer lots of entertainment: the giant building of the national cathedral with its great dome; the smell of the palm leaves and flowers resting on baskets for sale; the beauty of the National Palace peaking with its gardens full of gladiolus flowers and roses' blossoms; the stores and shops of "the portal walk;" and the music of Guatemala's national outdoor band shell. The auditorium was recognized with the name la Concha.

However, that day there were more people than usual at central park because people in the capital city were celebrating "Pagan parties" too before "Holy Week"; there were more street merchants and there were merchants selling carnival egg shells. These "eggshells" were time-consuming "crafts" that were created by imaginative minds. They had carefully chosen chicken egg shells, cleaned them, filled them with confetti of several colors, and closed/sealed them with colorful tissue paper. Then the outer shell was painted or decorated with a different color. The final product was a delight of creativity, ready for the entertainment of the consumer.

Then the crowd at the park were eager to participate in the pagan party but not Mercedes and Maruca. They remained sitting at a bench captivated by the hypnotic flow of water on the different levels of the national fountain. The huge fountain appeared as a big flower with its upper petals being washed with water. Suddenly, Maruca heard a crushing sound of paper, or cardboard, or crushing eggshells near her. And then she felt that something had fallen on her head or maybe a hand of a person had gently brushed her hair. And then, like two magnets, they were attracted to each other with a smile, as if they had agreed to meet exactly at that location.

The young man then started a conversation with Maruca and Mercedes. This person's hand had been subtle and with good judgment, without tangling Maruca's beautiful wavy hair that she had worked on herself that day. The young man had crushed the "carnival eggshell" in his hand just above Maruca's head, and had allowed the confetti to fall on Maruca's head without disturbing Maruca's hair.

Usually, this past custom in Guatemala was done by a young man trying to attempt to start a conversation with a young girl. Perhaps, he was shy or timid or did not know if the young girl felt the same way too. A young man would carefully break a "carnival eggshell" on a young girl's head, and the young man would hope the young girl would follow him and break an eggshell on him too. In other words, he would "break the ice" to start a conversation between them. But many times these were done roughly and in an annoying way to each other and then pretty soon people complained and the custom soon disappeared with the help of lawyers.

But that day at the park, when Maruca turned her head to look around her, she saw a young man with a clean haircut and a small mustache, wearing Sunday clothing and well-polished shoes, with black soft wavy curls of hair, smiling at her and with a cute Roman pencil nose. She smiled back at him, but she didn't want to engage with him by following silly pagan traditions. She was with Mercedes. She had not bought any carnival egg shells. She had not gone to the park to start a relationship with a young man. The young man instead apologized and requested to join Mercedes and Maruca by sitting on the bench and talking with them.

Presumably, the young man had worked up the nerve to talk to "las damas," Maruca and Mercedes. The "beautiful ladies by the fountain" allowed the young man to sit and talk with them at the bench. To Maruca La Chapina, the most attractive personality trait of this young man was not his pleasant looks, nor his well and clean clothing, nor his small mustache nor his black Superman hair with curls hanging from his forehead, nor his grime-free fingernails, but his speech, his words, his eloquence to communicate in the Spanish language with strangers at the national park—his dominance to express himself with confidence.

Later that afternoon, the young man persuaded Maruca and Mercedes to walk about two hundred meters to the national outdoor theater to the band shell which was surrounded by tall cypress trees. Maruca and Mercedes agreed to the idea of listening to music in a more calm environment, to a concert in Marimba instead of being close to the loud celebration of the pagan party being done by the fountain. Mercedes and Maruca appreciated the young man's advice since he seemed most informed of the festivities of the day at the national central park. Little did they knew, this was the start of the book of love of Maruca and Francisco's life together.

Maruca remembered the time back in Escuintla, when a young man showed up at their home to request her hand in marriage to Eugenio and Mercedes. She didn't know anything about the young man, and in addition, he had taken the freedom to bring some gifts to her parents. She was totally surprised and annoyed by this young man's audacity. After a meeting between Eugenio, Mercedes, and Maruca, the young man was informed of Maruca's disinterest on his proposal of marriage.

BIBLIOGRAPHY

A. K. A. God. *The Living Bible Paraphrased*. Wheaton, Illinois: Tyndale Publishers, 1971.

DHHS (NIOSH) Pocket Guide to Chemical Hazards. Publication no. 2005-149.

Lapworth, Katherine. *Get Your Book Published*. McGraw-Hill Companies Inc. (UK Company), 2010.

Lee, Christine. *The Oxford Paperback Spanish Dictionary*. Oxford, New York: Oxford University Press, 1993.

Perry, John. *Chemical Engineers' Handbook*. McGraw-Hill Book Company Inc. (USA).

Manual del Ingeniero Químico. México, 1976.

Recinos, Adrian. *Popol Vuh: "Las Antiguas Historias del Quiché."* México, 1946.

The World Book Dictionary. Chicago, Illinois: World Book Inc., 1988

Webster's New World Dictionary of the American Language. New York, NY: Warner Books Inc., 1982.

Webster-Merriam, Dictionary and Thesaurus. Springfield, Massachusetts: Merriam-Webster Incorporated, 2006.

Wildlife Encyclopedia. New York, New York: Funk & Wagnalls, 1974.

GLOSARIO GUATEMALTECO

A: es por atol de elote, con canela y granos de maíz; anís; aula; apazote (hierba comestible); antorcha; atún/tuna fish (pescado salado).

B: es por bichos (insectos); bacalao (pescado salado); "botran" nombre del rum nacional de Guatemala.

C: es por chompipe (ave); chiltepes; chiriviscos; chinchines (instrumento musical); chapina; chipilín; chicharrones; chirmol; chicharras (insecto); cazar; combinación (ropa interior femenina); cusha (licor maya); chucho (perro in maya).

E: es por escopeta (arma).

es por "Apoyó" an outdoor open wood fire off the floor—waist height with a tin roof; usually found in traditional well-to-do homes as a second kitchen in the city. But it is also found in simpler homes as their "only" place to prepare hot food, mostly out in the country. This second convenience had its own special set of cooking dishes. They were usually made of "clay" ("barro"), such as "comal" a flat thin platter to make tortillas, roast coffee, and roast dry spice mixtures. Jars or kettles were where "Guatemalan" tamales were steam, but also chuchitos, fry pork, or atol de elote. "Jarrones de barro" were good to make the special "chocolate drink" for family's birthdays.

es por "baile" ("dance").

F: es por flautas (instrumento musical); fustán (ropa interior femenina).

G: es por guaro (licor); güisquiles (vegetal); guacal es maya word for vessel to hold liquids, shape of coliseum; "gallo" el nombre de cerveza nacional en Guatemala.

H: es por honor; hembra; horchata (rice bebida guatemalteca).

I: es por la abreviatura "INRI" que significa en el idioma Latin: "Jesús el Nazareno, Rey de los Judios." La abreviatura que tenía la cruz de Jesús mandada a poner por Poncio Pilatos. Las otras dos cruces eran de dos ladrones y no tenían ningún signo o marca.

J: es por juilin (pez); jocotes marañones (fruta); "Jocón verde" (plato de comida guatemalteca).

L: es por latina y ladina.

M: es for marimba = a percussion (sharp blow) wooden musical instrument with an overall shape of descending/ascending musical tones, as a musical scale or chart. Typically, a standard marimba consists of a single or double row of eight or more notes. These notes are represented in the form of various sizes of wooden boxes protracted from the bottom (from large to small) with an endpoint shaped as pencil points or elongated teardrops. These boxes are held by strings and are open at the top. The open tops are nearly covered by several flat pieces of wood (from large to small) laying perpendicularly to the open tops. Also, these vertical keys or teclas (Spanish word) are positioned in an orderly manner (from large to small) by strings. Importantly, all pieces in this musical instrument called marimba are not supposed to come in contact with each other, so as to create unique sound notes. Finally, the delicate arrangement of all loose pieces of wood is protected by wooden walls with four (4) legs similar to a kitchen table. Then the keys or teclas are hit to make the "sharp blow" with a couple (two or more) of wooden sticks fitted with a rubber ball at one end. This wooden instrument is Guatemala's national musical instrument.

M: es por matate (bolsa); musgo; manicuro; mojarras (pez); marimba (nacional instrumento musical); macho; mapaches (racoon); madrileña (veil over the head to go to church); machete—the new "sword" at the New World mainly used for work.

M: es por Maya Quiché (tribu americana); Maruca; mestiza; es por muletas (crutches).

N: es por nances (fruta).

P: es por pascua; peruleros (vegetal); "pito" (instrumento musical); perraje; pitayas (fruta); pacayas (vegetal); petate; pizarrones;

"pishtones" (tortillas gruesas); pepián (plato de comida guatemalteco); pichones (aves); panela (azúcar café); es por petate (mayan word for mattress or sleeping bag).

P: es por Pedro de Alvarado (capitán, Conquistador Español de Guatemala);

Q: es por quetzal (ave); lenguaje o idioma "Mayan Quiché."

R: es por remolacha (vegetal).

T: es por tamalitos; tepocates; tata (Dios Padre); tecomate (recipiente); tecla; tarima; trombones. Mayan war god called tohil.

T: es por Tecún Umán (héroe y Cacique nacional Guatemalteco/Centroamericano).

U: es por unigénito (único), "Jesús" el hijo de Dios.

V: es por varilla.

V: es por virtue = a moral standard, a value, more at excellence.

Y: es por yuca (raíz de vegetal); yeso.

ACKNOWLEDGMENTS

First of all, I would like to mention God's continuing providence and promises to his people, to recognize without merit, his continuing love for past, present, and future generations in our family. My maternal grandparents were blessed with a fruitful eternal love relationship between them and God.

Eugenio and Mercedes's life together blossomed during an era of calamities and illnesses and without the conveniences of "modern" time gadgets. They were able to survive and were able to keep their love alive and vibrant between them for a long time. They walked together on the road of life, but they were not alone, God was with them. They always seek God over everything. Their road of life had many laughs but also had tears and disappointments, but they never gave up. They persisted while living near the Pacific Ocean at Escuintla, Guatemala in Central America.

Approximately between the years of 1900 and 1945, my maternal grandparents raised a family of two (2) children, while going through the heartbreaking and incalculable sadness of losing eleven (11) children. Standing on the promises of God and the hope of life everlasting, precisely on Jesus's resurrection, Mercedes and Eugenio lay to rest eleven (11) of their children with the anticipation of all of them reuniting in eternity again, with all their thirteen children.

Great gratitude goes to my parents who taught me about the importance of listening to the teachings of my family's elders and being able to see them as a source of wisdom and learn from God's past faithfulness. A time that was genuinely full of love, tenderness, faith, and hope. A celebration of the many times we spent listening, conversing, and appreciating the cool evenings at our house's patio, after dinner (in Guatemala's capital city, Guatemala). My father would play his wooden guitar to romantic folklore sonatinas/baladas but mainly to listen to what my maternal grandmother considered "Thanks to be God," a pastime, a good time, and a "happier time," but this time had its sad and painful episodes as well. Examples of God's never-ending "love" story.

I would like to acknowledge the "formal education" I received at the many professional and educational establishments located in Guatemala's capital city, Guatemala, starting from kindergarten school; primary school named "Colegio Loyola"; secondary school named La "Casa Central"; and tertiary schools named Colegio de Señoritas—"el Sagrado Corazón de Jesús," and the University of "San Carlos de Guatemala" Faculty of Industrial Chemical engineering. Great respect for all those instructors, teachers, nuns, priests, and professors, who spent hours preparing their teaching lessons to inspire (us) students to learn and appreciate the American history of our lives, under God's will, in relation to the entire world.

Lastly, it is without a doubt right to mention the encouragement and love that I have always received from my immediate family, especially my husband, William G. Bakker.

ABOUT THE AUTHOR

Julie Bakker was born and raised in Guatemala in Central America. She was educated in the country's Catholic school system, from second grade through high school. Then she attended the University of San Carlos School of Engineering. During the second year, she met her husband; they took their wedding vows and emigrated to the United States. Then they established a home in Indiana, raised a family, and she became a citizen. Meanwhile, she finished her college education at Purdue University with a degree in Industrial Engineering Technology with a minor in chemistry.